Praise for Souvenirs

"*Souvenirs from the Life of a Renegade Priest*, a delightful memoir, offers a picture of how irreverence and holiness can co-exist. Irreverence is most apparent where Jim Petty confronts religious and social convention. Holiness flows from the painful end-of-life stories Jim tells, where AIDS victims and God's other beloved "unclean" children meet his boundless grace, often embodied in other people. In this witty and moving book, personal misadventures are interwoven with heartrending reminiscence about pastoral care, epitomizing a gifted storyteller's art."

—Edward L. Bleynat, Jr., attorney and author of *The Synoptic Gospels: A Journey Into the Kingdom, Volume I: From Bethlehem to the River Jordan*

"Absolutely outstanding collection of wonderful vignettes; some heartrending, some joyous, some very funny—all instructional and inspiring."

—*The Rev. Anne C. Brower, M.D.*

"Father Petty's book is a must-have for clergy and *anyone* who appreciates the humor in church and pastoral life. His stories, many told on himself, point up both the fragility and resilience of the human contition—which, of course, is the *pastor's* condition, too! These terse and witty vignettes provide solace, laughter and godly admonition to anyone who dares to be a caregiver. I look forward to returning to these stories again and again in the hope that his down-to-earth and hard-won wisdom proves contagious."

—The Reverend Anne Gavin Ritchie, *Rector, Church of the Resurrection, Alexandria, Virginia*

Souvenirs

From the Life of a Renegade Priest

Ren·e·gade:

(ren′•ə•gād′) *n.* **1**. an individual who rejects conventional behavior. **2**. unconventional. <ML, *renegat(us)*>

Souvenirs

From the Life of a Renegade Priest

Rev. James S. Petty, M. Div.

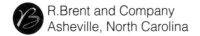
R.Brent and Company
Asheville, North Carolina

Disclaimer: Names, places and dates have been modified to protect the innocent from potential embarrassment and the guilty from accountability.

Published in Asheville, North Carolina by
R. Brent and Company
50 Deerwood Drive
Asheville, NC 28805
828-299-0977
E-mail: robbin@rbrent.com

Editor and Publisher: *Robbin Brent Whittington*
Cover Design: *jb graphics,* Asheville, North Carolina
Interior Design: *R. Brent and Company* and *Electronic Publishing Services, Inc.*
Compositor: *Electronic Publishing Services, Inc.,* Jonesborough, Tennessee
Author Photograph: *John J. Shea,* Reston, Virginia

Library of Congress Cataloging-in-Publication Data

Petty, James S.
Souvenirs: From the Life of a Renegade Priest—1st ed.
  p. cm.
  ISBN 0-9678061-3-5
  1. Autobiography 2. Religion 3. Humor
  Title
                          2004104998 LCCN
First Edition

2 4 6 8 10 9 7 5 3 1

Printed in the United States of America

This book is dedicated to:

Nancylee Bogardus Petty

The most important part of my world,
and the most important person in it.
With my best love and appreciation.

Contents

Trust

Family/Community

With gratitude for
The Right Reverend Robert H. Johnson,
Bishop of Western North Carolina.
You are truly my "Reverend father in God" who,
respecting my human dignity, welcomed me into my
retirement here seven years ago.

I will never forget you.

Thank you, Bob.

Jim+

James Petty
Black Mountain, North Carolina
July 2004

Introduction

've been collecting stories since I was seven years old. Here are a few of my favorite memoirs. Some are funny, some are tender; others are heartbreaking, maddening and disturbing.

"Do justice" and "love mercy." Those two commands sum up, for me, the essence of Jesus' value system, which he has left for his followers to adopt as their own. They have fueled my passion for what I've been about for most of my life. I've had my hands full trying to live them, and to my dying breath, that's what I'll be up to. I often don't get it right; sometimes I don't get it at all! After all, educated guesses are all any of us have about a man who's been dead for over 2,000 years! Thankfully, perfection has never been the requirement; only that we get up one more time than we fall.

I don't like bullies. Of any kind—corporate, ecclesiastical or bureaucratic. A bully is any institution or individual who profits from another's misfortunes, by exploiting, taking advantage of, harming, or devaluing another human being. (The German language has the perfect word for this: *schadenfreude.*) I want to side with those underdogs by advocating for them, and thwarting and exposing cruelty and hypocrisy when I see it. Jesus always sided with the unfortunates of this world. This means that he, and anyone who follows him, is at odds with the current "domination system"—a term invented by Walter Wink— in religion (the temple excesses), and the state (Roman exploitation of the Jews).

I learned early in life what it feels like to be bullied, so I can identify with others who have been exploited. My compassion is with—not for—society's casualties. I want to side with those who are easy targets for predatory humanity. So, often I advocate by using confrontation: through prophetic criticism, "perfect squelches," righteous indignation, and holy anger. Not just to get it out of my system (revenge), but also to be faithful to the model—the things that Jesus said and did. I don't think Jesus gives a diddily-squat what we "believe," as long as we believe that justice and mercy are a way of life. He's much more interested in what we do.

As Jesus said to his followers in *Luke*, "Why call me 'Lord, Lord' and do not do what I've told you to do?" I often wonder about my methods, and myself, but I do it anyway. Better to get it wrong than to stop trying. My intention is to follow Jesus' way.

Ten of my forty-four years' of ordained ministry were given to people with AIDS. I was a volunteer therapist with The Whitman-Walker Clinic for gay men in Washington, D.C. I wrote the first pamphlet on the microbiological risks of AIDS called, "AIDS and the Common Cup." Ministering among these folks was painful. They all died! I remember pulling off the road when I needed to cry, which was often.

Jesus is reported to have said, "Ye shall know the truth, and the truth shall make you free." Two thousand years later, a plaque at the entrance to the Virginia Theological Seminary library reads, "Speak the truth come what may, cost what it will." (Professor William Sparrow 1801–1874) To this day, the idea is alive and well.

In my ministry, I have often found myself saying things other people secretly agreed with but were reluctant to say themselves. They pretended to be shocked, but then told me privately that they were relieved to hear the truth on the table. I became the mouthpiece for what they couldn't say in public or in church. Maybe I encouraged cowardice on their part; or maybe I was a source of encouragement for them to speak the truth, too, … when they were ready.

And when life seems too serious, I try to remember that Jesus had quite a sense of humor. The comedic in his life reminds me not to take religious, cultural and familial prohibitions too seriously. Godly play has helped to keep me sane. I *know* God also must have a great sense of humor because, . . . well, I'm here and sometimes I'm all she has to work with. Maybe you, too. I've always been able to rely on humor to bring levity and hope to any situation. One step at a time. One day at a time.

James S. Petty+

Breathe on me breath of God,
Fill me with life anew,
That I may love what thou dost love,
And do what Thou wouldst do.

The 1940 Hymnal, #375
Edwin Hatch, 1878

Do
Justice

Almighty God, who hast created us in thine own image: Grant us grace fearlessly to contend against evil and to **make no peace with oppression;** and, that we may reverently use our freedom, help us to employ it in the maintenance of justice in our communities and among the nations, to the glory of thy holy Name; through Jesus Christ our Lord, who liveth and reigneth with thee and the Holy Spirit, one God, now and for ever.   Amen.

—Book of Common Prayer, #21,
Prayer for Social Justice, p. 209

Tiny

I was nine. Mom and I were walking down a side street in the small Virginia town where she was born. It was 1938. The sidewalk was narrow. A black man was standing on the sidewalk, blocking our way, just standing there with his back to us. We stepped down into the ditch to get past him, and were just stepping back onto the sidewalk when a loud crack, like a gunshot, whizzed past our heads. It was the snap of a bullwhip hitting the man's legs.

A red-haired, stubble-faced man in farmer's overalls yelled from the other side of the road, "You goddamn nigger, you step down when a white lady is on the sidewalk!"

The man rubbed his ankle. Suddenly my sweet, little, 96-pound mom—everybody called her "Tiny"—hurried across the street, snatched the bullwhip out of the red-head's hand, and hit him across the face with the handle saying, "A man is known by the way he treats his servants!" She threw the bullwhip at his feet, and we marched on down the sidewalk.

Lesson number one: Side with the underdog no matter how scary it is. We had a housekeeper/cook and a house boy. He taught my brother, Richard, how to jitterbug. She made the best biscuits in town. Also, Mom had a seamstress who'd bring her portable machine to the house and hem Mom's dresses, and make curtains and cleaning rags for her. All three were black. Mom treated them with respect, and as much equality as living in Virginia allowed.

Lesson number two: Respect the dignity of *every* person you ever meet. I must have internalized those two values early, because I recognized them in the behavior of a man named Jesus ben Joseph when I read about him later, in the Gospels, and felt right at home.

Licorice

*O*ur son, Steve, seven, loved licorice. I was at a clergy conference in Louisiana. In a souvenir shop, I found a replica .22 pistol made of licorice! It was hollow on the inside, like chocolate Easter bunnies. I got it for him, and put it in a paper bag on the front seat.

On the Interstate going home, some guy in a blue pickup almost ran me off the road, drifted behind, and then did it again! Deliberately! Pulling up next to me, grinning under his cowboy hat, he flipped me the bird and stared at me. So, I pulled out the black .22 and pointed it at him, right in his face, like they do on TV.

He jumped his pickup forward, like a rabbit, and disappeared.

Sensing he might car-phone for help, I ate the gun.

In about ten minutes, here they came . . . sirens and blue lights flashed me to the shoulder. Three officers approached my car, guns drawn. "We have a report that you threatened another driver with a weapon. Get outta the car." They practically strip-searched me; tore into the car like dogs trained to find drugs. While one officer was looking under the front seat, the other two had their heads in the trunk. I stood on the edge of the highway, jabbing my finger at my stomach and giggling to myself. I guess to give the passers-by a "hint" of what was happening.

They found nothing of course, but warned me that they were going to search the roadside, and if they found it, they'd issue a warrant for my arrest.

I later realized that it was a dumb thing for me to do. That redneck in the blue pickup may have had a gun of his own! After all, I *was* in the Bible Belt.

I never told Steve.

I guess I am now . . . honey.

Home Delivery

*I*n my mountain mission congregation, babies were often delivered on the kitchen table. Hopefully, the doctor from town made it by show time. For the birth of the grandchild of dear friends and parishioners of mine, the family sat in chairs arranged in a circle, watching and waiting. Two women held Hazel's legs up while the doctor rubber-gloved the infant's head into view.

Suddenly, the baby was propelled forward by Mom's final push, and he slid right through the doctor's hands and onto the floor. Without a moment's pause, the doctor scooped the baby up and onto the mother's tummy, and started wiping the infant's face off while musing casually, "Eighty-five percent of them do this." Everybody around the table nodded proudly, glad that theirs' was one of the majority.

The doctor knew that if it had occurred to anybody in the room that he'd made a mistake with Hazel's baby, it would only take one barrel from the shotgun standing in the corner to blow his medical head off.

And God help us, they named the boy "William," after the "heroic" doctor!

It was a good thing I wasn't there.

Gentleman

*Y*ou know how you can "sense" someone behind you? I was headed for the grocery store, and I sensed she was right behind me when I opened the door. As I stepped inside, I got a loud, sonorous, "Well...tha-nk yooou!" As I turned looked at her she said, "A gentleman would have at least held the door."

I just got my cart and moved into the aisles. Several times, we played bumper-cars around the end-caps and every time we met, she gave me a look that would have withered Genghis Khan. Finally, when we met at the frozen vegetables, I said, "Listen lady, if I heard you scream 'help!' or 'rape!' from down a dark alley at night, I'd run in and try to assist you. But I don't hold doors for able-bodied women as if they were the 'weaker sex' or something."

We met for the last time in the checkout line. I looked at her and guess what? She smiled at me!

Gay and a Marine Dad

rad was 28 and gay. I'd been seeing him in my office for several months. He'd been aware of his sexual identity since he was eight, and had struggled with it daily ever since. As a Christian, Brad wanted to stop pretending, and tell his parents the truth. After all, Jesus had said, "Ye shall know the truth, and the truth will make you free." (John 8:32) But he was afraid of his dad, a lieutenant colonel in the Marines. Dad was also a "born again" Christian. So, he asked me if the three of us could meet in my office. I was privileged to listen in while Brad sensitively gentled his father into awareness of his sexual orientation.

Dad's face tightened, his lips became a thin blue line, and through clenched teeth, he whispered, "Brad, why did you turn gay?"

"Look, Dad," he said, "I just told you I was queer, not nuts! Anybody'd have to be insane to choose to be homosexual in America today." They fought. They cried. Dad quoted Leviticus and St. Paul.

Finally Brad said, "Okay, Dad, I'll make a deal with you. I will obey God's word and act straight, if you think that's what God wants me to do, if you, too, will obey his word."

"Certainly, Son," Dad said as he leaned forward in the chair, "like what?"

"Go, and sell all that you have and give the money to the poor." (Mark 10:21)

Like the man in the original story, his dad went away very unhappy.

Bad-bad

I did a bad thing. I'd seen Giney for several months. Her husband, Matthew, broke her collar bone once, put her in the emergency room two other times with broken ribs, a sprained wrist and bruises. She always told the doctor that she fell down the basement steps or tripped over an electric wire. She won't press charges because she said, "I love him. I don't want him hurt. He's my husband."

Tuesday. Ten P.M. Giney calls me at home from her neighbor's. One eye is swollen shut, her lip is bleeding, and she asks me tearfully, "What can I do?"

"Hit 9-1-1 and ask for a policeman to come look at your face," I said.

"But I don't want to have him arrested!"

I reassured her, "You don't have to press charges, Giney, just let the cop take a report and I'll see you Thursday, okay?"

The officer showed up, looked at her face and said, "I'd just like to chat with your husband a moment." She took him next door where Matthew was watching a game with a friend. When they found Matthew, the officer asked, "Is this the man who did that to your face?"

"Yes," Giney said. As the officer cuffed Matthew, Giney protested, "I don't want him arrested; he'll kill me!"

"You don't have to bring charges lady, we will." In jail, an indignant Matthew loudly threatened to sue the police department, and to "take care" of Giney when he got home. The Assistant Commonwealth attorney said to Matthew, "Listen, if you lay a hand on her again, I'll personally phone your boss, lock you up and throw away the key."

The next morning, Giney met with an attorney whom I had recommended some time before. A female attorney. Matthew was released but he didn't go home. Giney's attorney advised him against that.

On Thursday, I asked Giney why she changed her mind about "protecting" her husband. She said, "When the officer hand-cuffed him and I saw the look on Matthew's face, for the first time I felt I had some power."

Giney proceeded with the divorce. She finally got the picture that God is not served by her staying in an abusive marriage. Nor does matrimony need to be a life sentence by a vengeful, rigid deity, for a youthful mistake in judgment. Just because she had "promised" to hang in "until death us do part," didn't mean she should stay around until he killed her! She didn't tell his boss about the arrest. If she got him fired, he wouldn't be able to pay child support.

On our last visit, Giney confronted me. "You *knew* the officer would arrest him without my filing a complaint, didn't you?" she asked

"Yes," I admitted, "I did a bad, bad thing."

As we hugged farewell, she said, "Yes, you did. Thanks."

Referrals

*R*ick and Marianne came to see me, disgusted with their previous five therapists, who they claimed, "didn't say anything . . . just sat there and grunted, or repeated what we'd just said in their own words." They wanted to know my credentials, and then they fought over them! Next, they wanted to know if I could see them on Saturdays at two, and asked, "What is the lowest figure on your fee scale?"

Rick deferred to Marianne when asked if my fee seemed fair, and then he fought with her for being wrong. When I started taking their history, he kept telling me hers, and she kept telling me his. About halfway through I gave up and said, "You deserve each other! I don't deserve either one of you! Why don't you find some other therapist to play games with?"

"Who're you gonna refer us to?" Marianne asked.

"I don't know any therapist that I'm that mad at," I said as I got up, opened the door and ushered them out, hoping that was the last I'd ever hear of them.

Wrong! New clients began calling who told me the same story. "We were at this cocktail party (church meeting, civic association, grocery store, etc.), and this couple began bad-mouthing this "Rev. Jim Petty who spoke so directly. He's not one of your nod-knowingly-and-say-nothing-therapists, like two-year-olds sitting on the potty and producing nothing but a simple grin."

These folks were getting pretty excited about a counselor who would actually risk losing clients in the service of telling them the truth as he saw it, so they called me for an appointment.

In the 14 years after I first saw Rick and Marianne, they sent me—inadvertently I am sure—11 new clients. Thanks!

By the way, I also learned from these new clients that, in fact, I alone was responsible for saving Rick's and Marianne's marriage. Any time they fight and it gets ballistic, they pause and say, "Well, Honey, it's a lot better than that goddamn Jim Petty!" They agree; they embrace; and live happily ever after.

St. Andrew

I founded St. Andrew Church. The first time I saw the church, it was a dog kennel with 45 residents! Six years later, the congregation was split over taking baby food and blankets to the folks at Poor Peoples March on Washington on the Ellipse. I went with some of my parishioners in their station wagons, which carried the supplies, because I thought their cause was just. That conscious decision on my part cost me my parish. The opposing group cancelled pledges and sabotaged parish programs until the day I resigned. The vestry called the bishop about a replacement. He promised to come meet with them the following week.

He brought the archdeacon with him. Not a good sign. When the vestry met with them, their first question concerned when they'd get a replacement vicar. The bishop said, "I don't intend to submit another of my clergy to this congregation. I've brought Dr. Davis to close this church and padlock the door, and you are invited to transfer to other nearby churches."

It stayed closed for several years until St. Mark's bought it and staffed it as a new parish mission. Today, standing on top of a hill surrounded by acres of lawn, it is a beautiful building which seats 500 people.

I was invited back to the church's 30th anniversary service. When Nancylee and I walked in the front door, there was a huge portrait of, guess who? The founding vicar! So I guess all is forgiven.

Now you know why I left parish work for pastoral counseling, and stand in awe of parish clergy today.

Professionalism

*S*ometimes I have to make a hospital call when I'm not "in uniform," like when I'm nowhere near home. Actually, when I'm in my tweed jacket and my salsa-red necktie, I look like a prosperous, successful, professional, middle-aged man, like a doctor. So from time to time, I drop in the local hospital's doctor's lounge. They have the *Wall Street Journal*. If a doctor comes in who knows me, I just hold up the paper so he can't see my face.

Today, a well-known heart surgeon dropped in for coffee. He began chatting with another surgeon, who said to him, "I hear you're going to do by-pass surgery on a 97-year-old woman tomorrow."

"Yep."

"Wow! Could I ask why?"

Without looking up from his travel magazine, he responded, "It's a billable procedure."

Some people seem to treat medicine as a commercial enterprise parading as a humanitarian profession.

Doctors

I've been in attendance with terminally ill folks a lot—40 year's worth. Doctor behavior at these times has been an eye-opener. First, about 90% of the time they are humane. The remaining 10% of the time, they are not, and I wondered why. Why some of them seem bent on refusing the patient's wishes about when "enough is enough," especially when the quality of life falls below acceptable limits for the patient.

Some refuse to remove life support, ignore patient's written wishes, and insist on using heroic measures to coerce unwilling victims to stay here. Why? You wouldn't insist that someone come to your house for dinner if they really didn't want to be there, would you? Why do a small percent of doctors insist that their will be done?

My observations suggest the following motives:

1. Money. As long as the patient has insurance, or an estate, everything medically possible is attempted to keep the shell breathing. I have noticed that when the patient, his family's finances, or insurance, runs out, these same doctors rapidly lose their resuscitation interest.

2. Religion. If respecting the patient's personal wishes conflicts with the doctor's private religious values—Roman Catholic, right-to-lifers, Fundamentalists, etc.— the doctor's personal religion wins out.

3. Insecurity. If the doctor's need for personal power over others means that he/she needs to 'have the last word,' the doctor's psychiatric fragility and emotional insecurity win.

4. Status. To preserve his/her image in the presence of other doctors, nurses, and hospital staff as the person "in charge" of the situation.

5. Fear. Fear of litigation. If he/she has the proper paperwork in hand, there's little to fear except the nuisance and publicity factor of an

unsuccessful suit brought by some remote family member who also wants to keep the patient here for his own personal reasons. Doctors' fear wins out over patient wishes.

6. Failure. Fear of failure, as if the patient's death is seen as a personal and professional failure for the doctor's self image.

7. Unfortunately, few bereaved families are going to bring suit against a physician who cared for their loved one. If, among the end-of-life papers, there was a letter to the family requesting that they use some of the estate money to sue doctors for "insufficient pain coverage," or "ignoring the patient's right to refuse treatment" at the end, maybe things would change.

isiting hours had not yet begun, but Bill was dying of AIDS and Marty wanted to be with his partner as much as possible.

As Marty stepped off the elevator, he heard screaming. It was Bill. Marty raced down the hall and rushed into the room where a doctor cooly told him to "wait outside." He didn't. They were performing the third spinal tap that day on Bill. The doctor was surrounded by residents and interns.

A nurse later told me she had objected, but the doctor said, "He's gonna die anyway, and these residents need the practice." Fortunately, Marty had Durable Power of Attorney. He yelled at the doctor, "You're fired! If you don't stop this procedure, I'll have you arrested for technical assault. Right now!"

Marty found another physician that day.

A human one.

"Catholic"

*T*he diocese was having a mass confirmation in a local cathedral. I knelt with everybody else and watched. What I saw nearly knocked me off the kneeler. The assistant bishop was delivering a stinging slap to the faces of each candidate in succession. I saw a small girl across the sanctuary watch the bishop slap her mother. The child looked up into her dad's face in shocked disbelief, but all Daddy did was grab her arm to keep her in the kneeling position. I'll never forget the look on that child's face: horror at seeing a man, a stranger, hit her mother in the face in front of 600 silent people. After the service, the little girl ran to her mother and clung to her protectively, the bishop's handprint still on her mom's face.

The next day, I wrote the diocesan bishop to protest what I'd seen. I've still got the letter of reply. He said that his assistant bishop was simply carrying out an ancient ritual called, not hitting, but "Episcopal Buffeting."

I wondered if "buffeting" could be an ancient rationalization for male chauvinism, or even worse, hidden sadism in both bishops? As always, the hierarchy closed ranks when challenged.

Attorneys are fond of saying that if a man slaps a woman once, it's his fault; twice, and it's her fault. But God help us, it was the women in the cathedral that day, especially the ordained women, who, by their silence, lent sanction to this clerical practice.

There's no use writing to the Association of Child and Family Therapists; or the American Association of Pediatricians; or the American Association of Clinical Psychologists; or even to the presiding bishop. They won't interfere with the inner workings of religion nor he with the inner workings of a diocese. I believe the Church came here to humanize the institutions of society. Now, the question is, who will humanize the institution of the church?

Carrie

y office phone rang early one summer afternoon.

"Hello, my name is Carrie Jacobs. I'm seventy-one years old. Do you think it's too late for me to get a life?"

"It's never too late. Why don't we get together and talk it over?" I replied.

"How old are you?" she asked.

"Sixty-three," I responded. "Why?"

"I just wanted to know if you're going to live long enough to help me."

"How 'bout Tuesday afternoon at five?"

"Okay."

"Do you drive?" I asked.

"Look," she retorted, "I just told you I was seventy-one, not decrepit!"

She began the session then and there on the phone. "I gave my whole life to my husband and children and he's dead and they might just as well be for all the time they spend with me."

"Where do you live?" I asked.

"I live in a ghetto. A Presbyterian retirement village. I'll die of boredom long before my heart stops beating."

This was going to be interesting. ... She showed up the following Tuesday. We started with her practical reality. She could read. She could drive. She liked children. In a few weeks, she was tutoring three disadvantaged grade-school kids in the Gum Springs area. Three times a week, after school. She was beginning to have a life.

One day, she told me that when she went to the doctor, she felt like a side of beef on an assembly belt: first being pushed into the doctor's office, then pushed into the examining room, then pushed out the door. "He never had time to listen to me or answer my questions," she lamented.

"Then," she went on, "one day my grandson, Jeremy, gave me his small tape recorder to keep. So I took it with me next time and put it on the doctor's desk saying, "You know, Doctor, I can't remember everything you say, so I thought I'd tape our appointment."

Each time she went to see her doctor, she took the recorder with her. "And you know," she said, "for some reason things changed. He started explaining the medications to me and their side-effects, and often said, "Now, Carrie, do you understand what I'm saying?" And he even showed me the X-rays of my joints! He acts like he has time for me now. I guess he's cutting back on his practice these days. "

"Great," I said, "and when you get home from your appointments, you just replay the tapes to be sure you didn't miss anything, right?"

"Oh no," she said, "the tape recorder doesn't work. That's why Jeremy gave it to me."

Learning
Curve

"O Lord where we are wrong, make us willing to change;
and where we are right, make us easier to live with. Amen."

Bellevue

*W*hen I was completing my clinical pastoral residency at Bellevue Hospital in New York City, I was given a master key to the psychiatric unit, a nine-story building somewhat apart from the other medical buildings. The floor signified intensity of pathology. Those on the first floor were only slightly disturbed people, like you and me, but as the elevator crept up, it got worse. The ninth floor housed the criminally insane, serial murderers and psychopaths.

I received a call near midnight that someone on the ninth floor had attacked another patient with a smuggled-in razor blade and asked if I would come and see if I could calm things down. I was half-asleep, but I jerked on my white coat, and headed for the hospital. When I got to the psych unit, I realized that I had forgotten my master key.

Fortunately, a nurse was going in the building at the same time, so it turns out I didn't need my key to get in.

After my visit with the two patients, I ended up being the one who needed to be calmed down. But both seemed better, so I left. When I got to the ward lobby and wanted out, I realized I needed my key. Several sleepless patients were shuffling around the dimly lit waiting room, glaring at me. I saw the charge nurse in her white starched dress and little Bellevue nursing cap. I told her I'd forgotten my key, and asked if she would please let me out.

"Nope," she said, and walked away.

"But I don't belong in here," I yelled after her.

"That's what they all say, hu-nee!" she cackled and poured herself a cup of coffee.

I was furious. Just then the chief of psychiatry came in and I went over and said, "I want to put that nurse on report. She's insolent!"

"Oh," he said, sucking on his pipe, "she's not a nurse. She just likes wearing the uniform. That way we don't have to give her as many tranquilizers."

He let me out.

Laity

*I*t was the bishop's annual visitation. Gladys Delaney cornered Bishop Goodwin at the coffee hour to bend his ear about her dissatisfaction with me, the former rector, as well as all of the other rectors that she'd ever known. He listened patiently, balancing our best china coffee cup on its saucer.

Finally, she finished, and waited for the bishop's response. "You're absolutely right, madam," he said, "the problem is that our only source for clergy is the laity."

Exams

*I*n 1959, I took canonical exams for ordination at the seminary. The liturgics practicum was held in the chapel. We had to practice administering the Bread. My examiner was Reno Howe, a hard-nosed kind of trickster from Richmond. But he did have a sense of humor. He *knew* that we hadn't been prepared for any of the Catholic traditions in the church. I put the little round disks that taste like cardboard (Grant Gallup calls them "Pennies from Heaven"), on the paten and started 'making rounds.'

Reno was kneeling at the altar rail with the rest of the students. When I got to him, instead of holding out his hands, palms-up, he stuck his tongue out at me! I had no idea what I was supposed to do, least of all place a wafer on his tongue. God knows where his tongue had been! The very idea seemed unhygienic, so I just stuck my tongue right back out at him, and moved on to the next person.

He insisted we do it all over again until we got it right, explaining that we should make sure the wafer gets into the mouth so it doesn't fall on the carpet and get desecrated. This time, I pressed the wafer firmly on the back of his tongue, apparently hitting his gag reflex, because he nearly vomited right there in front of everybody.

Anyhow, he must have passed me, because I did graduate.

Communion

*I*t was my first celebration of Holy Communion, a sweltering Sunday morning in July after it had rained all night. The setting was rural, and this meant that dressing up for church was the big event of the week.

You have to understand that Elsie always wore clothes that stood out. She liked to call attention to herself. This particular Sunday, she approached the altar rail wearing an outfit featuring a tight bodice, a deep, plunging neckline, and a huge, flowered hat. The brim of her hat was so wide that I couldn't see the chalice as it disappeared from sight, hopefully in the direction of her mouth. I didn't want to make a scene by asking her to remove her hat. After all, Saint Paul *had* said women shouldn't show up in church bareheaded.

The next thing I knew, she screamed and threw her head back with such force that the hat sailed off like a frisbee across the sanctuary. That's when I saw the red wine running down into her cleavage.

Now, I was really torn. On the one hand, I could hear the voice of Charlie Price, my old seminary professor saying, "If you ever spill the consecrated wine, just take the purificator and clean it up."

And on the other hand, I heard my mother's voice, "Don't you dare put your hand down there young man!"

Mother won.

Baptism

*T*he first baptism I ever performed was in a river, a rapid-flowing arm of the Shenandoah. I'd never heard of that before in the Episcopal Church, but lo and behold, the Book of Common Prayer actually *prefers* immersion to "pouring" or "sprinkling." (*See* BCP p. 307) In this remote place, they used the old Episcopal Missionary hymnal for revivals and services "in the field." About thirty folk were setting up for the after-baptism picnic. They began to sing, "Shall we gather at the river, the beauti-ful, the beauti-ful river," as they moved to the edge of the water.

I'd borrowed white hip boots from the local Baptist minister. (His church had a baptistery tank right in the sanctuary for winter use.) I slipped the white boots over my black clergy pants and waded in, beckoning the first of the two candidates to join me. Billy was a young man, recently converted. He and MayBelle, an older woman, were standing on the edge of the river, naked under their pure white robes. (*See* Revelation 7:13-17)

I cradled Billy in my left arm, and, as he sank backwards into the river, I said, "Billy Gray, I baptize thee in the name of the Father, and of the Son, and of the Holy Ghost. Amen." Then I lifted him up out of the water. It was a struggle. He splurted, and coughed and trembled and held onto me like a baby. But I knew he was "in the spirit," because he started crying.

I motioned for MayBelle, but she held up her hand like a traffic cop and declined, saying she'd rather "do it another day." Cold feet, I suppose.

The picnic was wonderful. Virginia Freeze made my favorite dessert, chocolate pie.

That evening I dropped in to see Lizzie Strickler. Lizzie chaired the altar guild and had "broken in" many a new deacon over the years. She was seventy-two and everybody's mentor. "How'd I do today, Lizzie?" I asked.

"Well," she said, "you did just fine. Still, I could make a couple of suggestions. First, if you lay 'em backwards upstream, the water don't rush up their noses when you pull 'em up, also, the force of the water helps you lift 'em up, instead of suckin' 'em back under. And then, you're supposed to pull 'em up out of the water after each of the three names, 'Father, Son, and Holy Ghost,' so they can git a breath in-between. You're not supposed to hold 'em under the whole time."

"Do you suppose that's why MayBelle changed her mind at the last minute?" I asked.

"I reckon," Lizzie replied with a smile.

First Wedding

*T*he wedding was held at The Falls Church, a prestigious colonial Virginia Episcopal Church. The rector was in England, and I was to officiate at the wedding of the only daughter of a well-known congressman. Stretch limos filled the parking lot, and the church was packed. Some people were even outside, watching through the windows.

Everything was very elegant. Flowers cascading throughout the church, a pure white silk runner adorning the aisle, brocaded ring-bearer's cushion, the church's finest antique sterling on display.

Then, in my most solemn voice, I petitioned Almighty God that this couple may be, "joyfully loined together," instead of, "lawfully joined together!"

For a second, I thought maybe they didn't hear me. Then the crucifer began a long stifled giggle. The acolyte's was anything but stifled. And it spread like a plague through the congregation until the whole place was in gales of laughter. I waited until it settled down and went on with the ceremony.

I had been expecting a big fat honorarium from Daddy.

Guess he forgot.

Burial

*I*t was my first funeral in the mountain missions, and the family cemetery was way up a steep rocky hill! The hearse that was bearing Grandpa went as far as it could, then the pallbearers had to haul the coffin the rest of the way up on foot.

Finally, the funeral director lowered the shiny mahogany casket into the ground. The family surrounded the open grave singing, "Will the Circle be Unbroken …?" Artificial green grass had been stretched over the bare earth around the edges of the grave.

I stepped forward onto the Astroturf. There was nothing under it! My feet hit the lower half of the casket with such force that the upper half-lid snapped open and dirt poured in onto Grandpa's face.

Here I was, on hands and knees, on the lower half of the casket, trying to brush the red Virginia clay off the man's face. I repeated, over and over, "I'm sorry, I'm sorry, I'm sorry," until I got the lid to snap shut again, and was helped out of the grave by the funeral director.

I tried to regain my composure, and my place in the Prayer Book, at the foot of the grave. I was afraid to look up and into the faces of the grief-stricken family … until I heard them. They were all shoving each other on the shoulders in paroxysms of laughter … the way people do when they don't believe what they have just seen, and find it hilariously funny.

Ninety-two

s a young deacon, I regularly visited the local home for the elderly. One Sunday afternoon, I asked Edna, "Mind telling me how old you are?"

"Ninety-two," she said.

"Gee," I heard myself saying, with all the tact of the newly ordained, "I can't imagine living that long."

"Wait 'til you're ninety-one, young man," she shot back.

It's not seminary that teaches you parish ministry, your people do!

Fig Leaf

*I*t was early autumn. 1968, I believe. Still warm in D.C. I'd only been a pastoral counselor for a couple of years.

I read an ad about a workshop on relaxation massage for counselors and psychotherapists. So, I sent in my fee and registration form. I got a letter back with directions to a large house in northwest Washington, suggesting I bring a towel with me. That was reassuring.

I knocked gingerly, half-hoping they wouldn't hear me. A woman stuck her head around the door. She was very pretty, with long, sandy-colored hair, and a string of peace beads around her neck. She gave me a big smile and, in her Alabama hospitality voice, said, "Hi huni, c'mon in. Mah name's Apple." She closed the door and I admired her beads ... she had nothing else on that I could safely admire. I had a sudden impulse to fling open the door and scream my way back to my car, but obediently, like a sheep following the shepherdess, I trailed her derriere down the hall to a large, paneled recreation room.

There was a cozy fire in the fireplace, and fifteen people—nine men and six women—were standing around, fully "clothed and in their right minds." (Mark 5:15) They were pretending to be chatting with each other, towels in hand.

Soon, the leader appeared. He has his clothes on, too, thank God. There were eight massage tables around the perimeter of the room, draped in white sheets ... like you see at the morgue. He asked us to sit down, and then explained that we'd be selecting a partner and getting two hours of individually supervised practice in the art of massage. We would then switch places for another two hours. All of this would be followed by an especially healthy supper of organically grown foods, prepared by, of all people, Lady Godiva herself.

Next, the leader suggested we find a spot in the room to undress and to leave our things in one place. There was a slightly elevated nook about as far away from the others as I could find, so I went up there and, along with everybody else, faced the leader who was in the center of the room with Apple. We watched him intently for our next instruction. First, he took off his right shoe, then left shoe. Off mine came. His right sock, then left. Then mine. Then he peeled off his T-shirt. Me, too.

As he unbuckled his belt, I just "knew" he had a swimsuit underneath. Wrong! Jockey shorts. Hanes, in fact.

The women removed their brassieres. I took off my trousers. And again, I had an incessant urge to escape. But everybody else removed their last items, so I turned my back to them and complied, standing there looking down at my feet. And then I looked up. I was standing naked, directly in front of a floor-to-ceiling picture window that faced onto Pine Street. People were walking up and down the sidewalk. Five feet away. I quickly wrapped the towel around me and joined the group, only to find out that I was the only one who had put the towel on. Turns out the towel was for rubbing the massage oil off each other in-between shifts, not to hide behind.

"Choose partners!" came our leader's cheery command. "Would anybody choose me? Would I dare choose the person I really wanted to work on?" I had little time to decide. A hand placed squarely on my shoulder settled the matter. His name was Tom. After he'd poured almond oil all over me and started working, I wondered who he was mad at. Luck of the draw. Wouldn't you know I'd get a psychopath. Soon, it was my turn! By then, I'd discovered the difference between being naked and being nude. Being nude means you just don't have any clothes on. Naked is how you feel about being nude if you were brought up Roman Catholic or Southern Baptist.

Finally, it was over. Like an instructed Eucharist, the leader had walked us through every step, explaining what we were supposed to feel. Then we all toweled the oil off each other, said our "thank-you's," and headed—at least I headed—for my pile of clothes. But not so fast . . . we were supposed to have lunch first, sitting in a circle so we could see the after-glow effects of the toweling on each other's skin. So I turned around and quickly rejoined the group . . . or almost. . . .

Uncle Tom had neglected to towel the oil off the bottoms my feet and I slipped and slid right for the fireplace, on my back, scattering the fireplace tools. Apple and the leader rushed to help me up.

After I'd regained my footing, we sat cross-legged in a circle, facing each other, in front of the fireplace. We were told to assume the "lotus position" with our feet twisted upside-down and locked on the inside of our thighs . . . like those little statues of Buddha you see. Agony.

Enter: Apple, with huge chunks of sesame-buttered Russian black bread, and wooden bowls filled with steaming-hot lentil soup. My legs were numbing, but I kept smiling and pretending that I assumed this position three times a day. The man directly across from me was having a harder time. I could see the jugular veins in his neck bulge as he strained to keep his heels dug into his crotch. He started blowing on his soup spoon when his greased right foot lost it, and snapped out of place, tipping the bowl of scalding soup backwards onto his unprotected, no-longer-"private" parts. He jumped up, screaming, dancing on one foot and then the other with his fingers outstretched like they could break off backwards.

We got him into the bathroom and onto the toilet, and it was like a fire brigade. We lined up with paper cups, coffee mugs, and flowerpot saucers— whatever we could quickly get our hands on—filled with cold water from the sink and, one by one, we poured the soothing coldness down his . . . ah . . . lower abdomen. It was like bringing libations to the king, only without genuflecting. Suddenly, I remembered that I had some spray Solarcaine in my car from the beach, and without a thought beyond emergency rescue, I rushed out to get it, feeling somewhat like St. Mark, and then I sprayed . . . uh . . . the area . . . which brought him great relief.

After supper, we did the "ohm" word, exchanged phone numbers, hugged one another all around, got dressed, and left.

Collar

*T*he trouble with my clerical collar is that I sometimes forget I have it on. I was at the checkout register in the grocery store last week, in a hurry to get to the hospital. The clerk handed me my bag of cookies and .97 cents in change. I dropped the change into my pants pocket. With the fistful of coins already in there, that was the last straw! I knew a hole was wearing down there but kept putting off fixing it. Coins rushed down the inside of my pants-leg, spewing all over the floor.

"Oh Shit!"* I yelled. Suddenly the place was filled with a heavenly silence. Even the cash registers stopped ringing. I was the object of a thousand silent "shame-on-you" looks (I was already on my knees for God's sake, what else did they want?).

A still, small voice whispered down from above the fluorescent ceiling panels, "They wanted you to live up to their expectations son, that's what!"

*P.S. The spell checker on my computer works fine, except that it didn't recognize the word "shit." It came up with "shift," "skit," "spit," "sit," "shad," and "ship," but no "shit." Must be Methodist software.

Souvenirs

Juice

My study was a small room added onto the vicarage. I could enter it through the kitchen, but it had a separate outside entrance for the public. I'd get up early, grab a large glass of orange juice and shut myself up in my study to work on my sermon without interruption.

Friday morning, 8:45. Pam calls. She's my Sunday school superintendent, weekly bulletin editor and mimeographer, chair of building and grounds committee and hostess for the coffee hour. Trouble is, when she opens her mouth, she's like a Mack Truck stuck in double-low, without a driver. Nothing stops her. Twenty minutes. Thirty minutes. Orange juice long gone. I needed to go to the bathroom, but nobody, nobody, interrupts Pam.

The need got stronger, and since my large empty glass was there, I . . . well, . . . I . . . (Later, the doctor I called for advice about my situation told me that it wouldn't hurt me.). Pam kept on for another 15 minutes and then said, "So long." Maybe she had to go, too!

Seminaries are famous for overlooking the dynamics of real parish life. I learned the hard way not to exploit hard-working parishioners, like Pam, who wanted to use the church and clergy to solve their personal problems. I learned too late for Pam and her husband.

In the fall, when the drill was about to start up all over again: Sunday school, building and grounds, coffee hour, weekly bulletin, and altar guild, the vicarage doorbell rang. It was Pam. She handed her church keys to me, and announced that she and Frank were divorcing, and she was returning to her mother's in Montana, and that, "No," she didn't want to talk about it. Two days later, she was gone.

The next week, I met Frank, who never came to church, in the grocery store. I asked him what happened. He told me Pam had been having an affair. "It destroyed our marriage years ago," he said.

Shocked, I asked, "Who was she having the affair with?"

"The church," he said.

(P.S. She had often said that she did all this church work because she "loved the Lord." Turns out the real reason was that she was avoiding her husband and an ailing marriage. Doing church work has always been an unassailable reason for not dealing with reality. I realized my complicity in their divorce by allowing, even welcoming, the "Pam's" of this world.)

With a little more experience and maturity, I would have said, "Pam, I'm going to hang up now. Call me tomorrow, okay?" (click!)

Thanksgiving Ticket

$\mathcal{S}$ome years ago, I was invited to celebrate and preach in a small church in a little town way down in Virginia. The rector was in California with his wife for the Thanksgiving holiday, visiting her parents.

The service was at 10 A.M. I had overslept and was late, so I was speeding to the church.

Soon, flashing red lights appeared in my rear-view mirror. I thought to myself:

1. Surely he will notice that I, *too,* am in uniform—going to do a good deed on a national holiday.

2. Surely he wouldn't want me to tell the whole congregation that he was the reason I was late.

He was pleasant enough. And he gave me a ticket. At announcement time, I told the congregation that I was late because I had overslept. ("Ye shall know the truth and the truth will make you. . . . ah . . . more truthful.") So, I came clean.

I also commended the people of that town for having a police officer who upheld the notion that nobody is above the law.

The next week I got a note:

Dear Rev. Petty,
Thanks for the promotion. The move from Sergeant to Lieutenant is quite a big jump. Sincerely yours, . . .

It was from my arresting officer. How could I have known that the chief of police was sitting in the congregation that morning?

Love
Mercy

"Dear God, May what we like about each other overcome what we don't like, lest we miss your beautiful face in … their eyes. May we see each other, the way you see us. Depart in peace."   Amen

Do-gooder

I read about respite care for families of developmentally disabled people. Parents who need a little time off to recover from the demands 24/7. They must be chronically exhausted. That pressed all my messianic rescue buttons.

That's how I met Stephan. He was 17, 6' tall, and weighed 160 pounds. He was very bright, had sparkling blue eyes, and a great sense of humor. That helped a lot with his clumsiness. While he could partially dress himself, it took him six minutes to tie his shoes, and he needed help with his personal toileting, bathing, dressing, and eating. He had trouble brushing his teeth without perforating his cheek.

When he walked, he'd drag the top of his right foot behind him and flail his arms uncontrollably. When he talked, it sounded like he was chewing his tongue. His throat muscles and carotids bulged and his nasal speech made him hard to understand.

Dad had left long ago, and Mom was worn out. She needed someone to give her a break on occasional Saturdays or weekends. On our first outing, he got in the car and I automatically proceeded to buckle him in. He frowned at me, unbuckled the belt and led me by the hand around the car. After pushing me into the driver's seat he proceeded to buckle my seat belt! Then he fairly danced around the car with glee, trying to clap his hands.

First we went to the mall. He managed the escalator better than I feared. In the department store, I got side-tracked by some item, and when I looked up, he wasn't there! I panicked and ran through the store until I finally found him—flailing his arms through the crystal stem ware section of the fine china department! Somehow, he knew the limits of his reach.

Then on to the ice-cream shop. He liked vanilla. I got his bib adjusted and spoon-fed him slowly (my aim was better than his). The way he handled being stared at was to flash a huge smile and floppily wave at his fascinated beholders. That made them look away from their own embarrassment.

He indicated his need to go to the bathroom the way all kids do. I let him go into the men's room by himself. Pretty soon, guys were running out like angry bees in flight formation! I investigated, and found Stephan staring at men at the urinal, then flinging open the toilet doors and yelling, "You making pretties?"

I brought him home that evening. While his mom was thanking me, Stephan gave me a big hug. It hurt. He didn't know his own strength.

As I was driving home, I asked myself, "Who was the teacher and who was the student? Who got the most fun out of that day? Who was neighbor unto whom?" I felt pretty fortunate.

Holy Communion

*L*ast Saturday night, the phone rang at nine. "Hello Father Petty, my name's Jared. You don't know me, and I don't have any right to call. I haven't been to church since I was a kid, but the person I love most in this world—his name is Rusty—is dying of AIDS and he'd like to have Holy Communion and to receive last rites. Is there a priest in the diocese of Virginia somewhere who might come do this for us?"

My mind wandered back to my seminary days. I was sitting in George's office again. The phone rang, and this is what I overheard: "St. Mary's Church, good morning! No, Cohen's grocery store is just down the street. Oh, it's not the 'wrong number'; it's never a mistake to call the church. Call again sometime. You have a nice voice."

Was it a mistake for this young man to call the church in time of need? Had he stayed away from church too long? I phoned three of my fellow clergy. Two wouldn't. One couldn't (or so he said). So I went. I was glad I did.

I found Jared and Rusty in the hospital room. Rusty could only nod a shy smile as if he were embarrassed to be dying. Jared started crying when I went over and greeted Rusty with a kiss. There were four other young men in the room. Silent. Friends. One still sullen because the church had not made him feel welcome when he was a kid, because he was "different."

Last rites. Laying on of Hands. Anointing with holy oil: "I do sign and fix thee with the sign of the cross, Rusty, in sure and certain hope of the resurrection of the body and the life everlasting." The oil glistened on his forehead, his chest, his palms and tops of his feet. The miniature gold chalice barely sufficed for the seven of us.

Afterwards, we held hands in a circle around Rusty's bed, Jared on his right hand, his best friend on his left, and me at his anointed feet. Each in turn spoke softly about some past experience with him, or reminisced about some things they did (and didn't!) like about him. Each began with, "Thank you Rusty for the time when we. ..."

When my turn came, I thanked him for inviting me to his farewell party. It was a celebration of life, of death, and life again.

Rusty entered a coma that night, and he entered the kingdom just before dawn the next morning.

A few weeks later, Jared came to see me. "The sign out front says, 'The Episcopal Church welcomes you.' Would that be true for me if I wanted to come back to the church again?"

"Probably not," I answered. "If 'the secrets of all men's hearts' around here should be opened, many of *them* wouldn't be welcomed either!

"The difference is that your secrets are no longer hidden. On balance Jared, I think you have 'chosen the better part.' Welcome home, son."

"*If* our hearts condemn us, God is greater than our heart and knoweth all things." Jn 3:20

This is the neat thing about God. When I do something bad, since he knows all things about me, including the good things, it's not so bad! Must be the mixture God loves. God is not neurotic. God does not love us when we're good and hate us when we're bad. Else we could ruin God's day! That's Power! Good and evil, like the tares and wheat must grow together in this life, until the harvest.

The coexistence of good and evil in us is reflected collectively in the ancient wisdom of the church. The "Articles of Religion" are tucked away in the back of the Book of Common Prayer, but not to worry, even if you could find them you can hardly read the print without a magnifying glass. Article xxvi reads, "... In the visible church the evil be ever mingled with the good." You see, the church knows that God understands something about us that other people don't always see. God knows that there is a difference between doing a bad thing, and being a bad person.

There are two types of people in this world: those who divide people in "types," and those who do not. In the world that raised me, people were divided into "good people" and "bad people." The good people were called "nice" and the bad people were called "naughty." Remember?

But what I'd been taught didn't match what I observed as I grew up. I saw some very good people doing some very bad things, and I saw some very bad people doing some very good things. It was confusing. And then one day I came across a poem. I don't know who wrote it, but it said, "In men whom men pronounce as ill, I find so much of goodness still, I hesitate to draw the line, where God has ... not."

Funny the way things turn out. Remember when you were a kid and your mom warned you not to associate with certain of your little friends she didn't approve of? Well, lo and behold, I have grown up to become one of those very people my mother warned me not to play with. Wasn't fair anyhow; she never asked me what I thought of her friends.

It soon became clear to me that you couldn't tell from the outside whether people were good or bad, so I began a kind of adolescent philosophical questioning of people's secret motives for what they did. I was soon hopelessly lost in the cotton-candy pietism of this one, until Canon Bryan Green, the great Anglican evangelist who came from London to the football stadium at Washington and Lee High School on a preaching mission. (Every now and then, the mother country sends a spiritual "care package" to the colonies to help stave off our predilection for self-destruction.)

One evening after the mission, I asked Canon Green about my concern. He said, "Son, if I waited for a pure motive to come along before I did something, I'd never do anything."

That helped.

"Lighten-Up"

 found Michael in Alexandria, on a mattress in the town-house basement of an attorney friend, who had taken him in over the Fourth of July weekend.

Michael had AIDS, Kaposi's Sarcoma. The purple lesions had blossomed all over his body. He couldn't work anymore, and had lost his apartment and everything in it. I'd drop in on the way to my office, or on the way home in the evenings. Michael was such a courageous, warm, good-humored, sensitive man. I really loved ministering to him as priest and friend.

I had just given a talk at St. Dunstan's Church about my AIDS ministry. At coffee hour afterwards, a man on my left warmly grabbed my hand, but on my right, no hand. In fact, this man turned his back to me, thrusting his right hand into his pants pocket. He even avoided looking at me.

Now, after six years of working with people with AIDS, this kind of treatment usually just rolls right off my back. But that day it got to me. Maybe I was tired, or fed up with some peoples' hate and fear. (As if he could get AIDS from a handshake!) I felt embarrassed and humiliated. Suddenly, in the midst of a room full of people chatting noisily, I felt like an outsider. Alone. And very angry. I couldn't take it anymore, so I left.

I knew that Michael would still be awake. (Seriously ill people don't sleep on our schedule. They often alternate between naps and being fully awake.) He looked worse that night, but alert. I sat next to him on the mattress and found myself saying, "Michael, I've got to tell you something. If I keep it in any longer, I'll explode." And I told him what had happened at church and how perfectly awful I felt.

He listened patiently, like any good pastoral counselor might, until I finished my story. Then he said, as his eyes flashed at me, "Now Jim, if you're going to hang around people who are being shot at, you're gonna catch a few stray bullets in the ass. C'mon now buddy, lighten up!"

I started crying. I wondered who ministers to whom in this ministry?

After church the following Sunday, I stopped and got him a lime soda, which seemed to help with the dryness in his mouth. But as soon as I saw him, I put the soda on the floor and took him in my arms. He held onto me tightly at first, and then slowly, very slowly, loosened his grip until he finally let go of me … and life.

The words echoed from the cold basement walls,

"Into thy hands, O Merciful Savior, we commend your servant Michael. Receive him into the arms of your mercy, into the blessed rest of everlasting peace. Amen."

Lizzie

I've been doing Meals on Wheels for shut-ins. It's one of the most satisfying things I do. There's an affinity in human suffering not otherwise commercially available. No self-pity, no blaming, just one foot in front of the other and a smile at the colorful sunset. I get to do a lot of "spiritual" things like, well, Lizzie's on my route. She lives in a run-down trailer in a run-down trailer park. She's 87, has had strokes, diabetes, dizziness and needs a walker to get around. Last winter I noticed the snow was left undisturbed. She doesn't have many visitors.

Her best company is "Sweetie," a 60-pound long-haired dog of mixed lineage, with warmly piercing eyes. She's one of these dogs that 'smiles.' But she growled and got between Liz and me the first time I visited.

When I delivered Liz's dinner, I noticed her toenails. They were two inches long and curled like spaghetti. It must have hurt her feet and in time would deform them. So next time I went, I took some clippers with me and began clipping 1/8th of an inch a week, which gave me an excuse to visit them more frequently. Sweetie allowed me.

As I started to leave last Wednesday, Liz whispered, "I think I messed up my bedroom." So I took a look. The orange shag rug next to the bed was splattered with vomit. I got a bucket and stuff to scrub it up, but I couldn't. It was hard and glossy like varnish. She had gotten sick two weeks before but hadn't mentioned it. So I had to get some really hot water and re-hydrate the vomit before I could even clean it up. Ever re-hydrated vomit? Anyhow, here I was on my hands and knees, Liz lying on her stomach across the bed, with her chin in her hands, peering over the edge. Sweetie was sprawled in the doorway, watching every move, and the three of us listening to opera on her boom box, Aida!

What a picture!

Funny, Liz tells me Sweetie doesn't usually let anybody else touch her, but when I do her pedicure, she readily puts her paws in my hands like an old friend. Guess I am.

Driving home, I felt so peaceful. Not smugly self-satisfied, more like I get to be with two people I love. [Sweetie's a 'people' to me, too.]

Rick

I visited Rick in his Georgetown townhouse. The Whitman-Walker Clinic for gay men had asked me to drop by. Interesting guy. His Harley was parked out front, and I had heard music on the way in. He was playing a studio grand Steinway. Brahms. He sported a butch haircut, and fading signs of being over-muscled at one time. He had "Leather" magazines on the coffee table, along with a sterling silver flute. He couldn't play the flute anymore; his cough was getting too bad.

His parents, who lived in Georgia, had kicked him out of the family years ago. He had been an engineer, and apparently from his surroundings, a successful one. We visited. Later, when he was admitted to Georgetown University Hospital, I visited with him many times. His parents' lawyer had told the hospital not to allow Rick's lover of fourteen years to visit him there. The hospital complied. There was a "Family Only" sign on his door. Once, the nurse questioned my visiting and asked, "Are you family?"

"Yes," I said, "he's my *brother* in Christ. Or maybe his mother's lawyer would like to take on the whole Episcopal Church in court!" (I knew my clerical collar would come in handy someday.)

Rick wanted his diary from his condo, so he gave me the key. When I got there, a large truck was moving the piano out. I protested! His dad responded by handing me a court order which stated that the family's interest took precedence over "outsiders." I couldn't even get his diary. I stood there on the 34th street sidewalk and watched them take out his stereo system, the silver flute and some furniture. I cry a lot in this ministry.

Two weeks later, St. John's, Georgetown, allowed me to conduct Rick's funeral there. His lover and friends all participated. His parents didn't show up. … Though they would have been welcomed. That's the Anglican Way.

"Blackie"

etween the 1963 Poor People's March on Washington, and the riots following the murder of Martin Luther King Jr. in 1968, D.C. was no place to be. I sloshed through the mud with Ralph Abernathy, visiting folk from further south in their plywood A-frame shelters on the Mall. The church's junior warden, with his new Checker Station Wagon, coordinated caravans from my church to what they called, "Resurrection City," on the ellipse, taking baby food and blankets into the troubled tent city.

One day I got a call. There were two women and three children trapped in their house in Anacostia. Snipers on the rooftops were firing sporadically, day and night. Several of the church families had agreed to house these folks until it was safe for them to return home.

I called on several families to help, and they agreed. At Chain Bridge, we were halted by an Army Reserve soldier with a carbine across his chest. "No one's allowed to go into D.C. It's too dangerous." I told him we had ministry for Jesus to do in there, and he could either shoot me or step aside. We shifted into first gear, and the soldier backed off.

We found the street. As we were looking for the house, I saw a man in a bright Hawaiian sports shirt carrying two paper bags of groceries down the street. It was Fr. Bill Wendt, rector of St. Stephen's and The Incarnation. He didn't seem a bit afraid.

We located the house. As we got out of the car, bullets whizzed by, almost grazing my head. Several pinged the "No Parking Sign" in front of us. (Who thinks about parking tickets at a time like this?) We found the women and kids, and loaded them into the station wagon. We had gotten about three blocks away when the little boy started crying.

"What's wrong son?" I asked.

"Blackie's back there, he's in the closet. He'll starve."

"Who's Blackie? " I asked.

"My new puppy."

"Turn around," I said.

"Have you lost your fucking mind completely?" the driver shouted.

"Turn around," I yelled, "I'll go in and get it."

The boy ran inside with me. We scooped the little thing out of the closet and ran back. As I was getting back into the car, more bullets zinged close by. I snuggled the whimpering pup on my lap. We left town as fast as we could. When we got back to Chain Bridge again, I waved a "thank you" to the soldier. As we were crossing the bridge, I breathed a sigh of relief. "Well done, folks!" I said, as I felt a kind of warm glow in the pit of my stomach. I thought it was the Holy Spirit. Turns out it was the puppy. Maybe, it was both.

Giddyap

His mom had been taking six-year-old Vinney to a child psychiatrist for months. Vinney's dad died of a heart attack the year before, and now the boy was constantly moping around the house unresponsive, and often quietly staring off into space.

The doctor said it was simply a grief reaction to the loss of his dad. But Vinney got worse, and when the psychiatrist suggested that he was autistic and needed medication, his mom thought she'd first try some other avenues.

At her pastor's request, I met with them and learned that on the fateful night, Vinney had been in his parents' king-sized bed with his dad, watching TV and eating popcorn until it was time for Vinney to go to bed.

Around 3 A.M., Vinney was suddenly awakened by flashing red lights outside his window. He opened the door a crack and peeked into the hallway, just in time to see two men rolling his dad quickly down the hall on a little bed. Daddy looked strange, ashen, and very still.

Next thing Vinney knew, Mrs. Bancroft, their next door neighbor, was there to stay with him while Mom was at the hospital. Dad had just had a physical, which he had passed with flying colors.

He died shortly after arriving at the emergency room. Of a myocardial infarction, a "sleeper," they called it.

Talk therapy doesn't work with kids as well as play therapy. After we'd gotten to know each other a few weeks, I started roughhousing with Vinney, using the office pillows on the floor. I got on all fours and invited him to "ride horsie," as kids like to do. He climbed on, grabbed my necktie for reins, started to say "giddyap" and then suddenly stopped, quietly climbed off, and busied himself with other toys scattered around the floor. His reaction was too sudden, too deliberate.

For his next session, I had the TV set up. I put cushions together on the opposite wall so we could watch Looney Tunes together. I even brought popcorn. But Vinney didn't want any.

Distracted by the TV, Vinney responded to my questions, and it came out that when he was in bed with Dad watching TV, during commercial breaks, he'd jumped on Daddy's chest and ridden horsie until the show came back on. That night however, Dad told him he was "too rough on Daddy's chest," and should just sit beside him for awhile and eat popcorn. Mom was in the kitchen and hadn't heard that exchange.

It wasn't just that Vinney missed his dad, Vinney's grief was secondary to guilt! He thought he'd killed his own dad playing horsie on his chest. Quite a burden for anyone, much less a kid, to carry around.

I suggested that Vinney's mom make an appointment with the cardiologist who saw her husband that night in the emergency room. He had taken a chest X-ray and a few minutes of EKG tape before her husband died. The doctor showed the tapes and film to them, explaining that this kind of heart attack gives no warning, and is not affected by outside exertion. Dad would have died that night, at that time, even if Vinney had been spending the night with a friend.

At our next session, I invited Vinney to help himself to popcorn while we talked. He finished most of the box. I knew this was our last session.

Cynthia

One morning in early fall, Cynthia called at nine and said, "I've got to see you right away. Can I come over now?"

"Yes," I responded, hung up, and canceled my next two appointments.

Twenty minutes later she walked into my office. Cynthia was divorced, working, and living alone with Meredith, her four-year-old daughter. She had had a dinner party the night before for a few friends. She'd promised herself that she would put the security cover over the pool now that it was getting too cold to swim. But she decided to put it off until after the party.

While the guests were having a good time in the living room, Meredith apparently wandered out the back door and fell into the pool. They found her facedown on the bottom some time later.

I held Cynthia in my arms while she sobbed uncontrollably for twenty minutes. Talk about blaming yourself. She wanted to die. To be with Meredith so she could say, "I'm so sorry for what I did." How could she live with this? She couldn't. She began that morning trying to turn it over to God. It took over a year for her to do that. But in the end, she had to let go of the crippling grief because she couldn't hold onto it anymore. Yet, by letting go, Cynthia was able to turn tragedy into blessing.

She began working with pool builders and developed a very explicit handbook for pool safety, even lobbied for some very important precautions that protected children to be adopted as County regulations. Nothing can bring Meredith back. But in the act of recognizing that we are not alone with the pain we cannot endure, we are able to transfigure life's impossibilities into blessing for others.

We'll never have to face anything alone. Ever again. We can now live with the worst life can do to us.

Thanks be to God. Amen.

Pinocchio

he rhyme from *Goldilocks* sang through my head and my feet as I skipped down the sidewalk to the woods.

"This porridge's t-o-o h-o-t.

"This porridge's t-o-o c-o-l-d.

This porridge's j-u-s-t r-i-g-h-t!"

I was ten years old. Somebody had looped a steel telephone cable over a branch, high in an ancient oak tree. You could swing way out and "plop" right down into the middle of the pond.

My mom was good to me. T-o-o g-o-o-d. She was too warm.

Dad was distant. He was t-o-o cool.

An' nobody ever showed up (except maybe Grandma) who was j-u-s-t r-i-g-h-t.

On the last block, just before you got to the woods, lived Mr. and Mrs. Madden. They were Irish. I used to see them go to early mass on Sunday mornings. She wore a lacy black shawl over her head and sometimes carried a red rose bud in her hand. God didn't give them any children. Mrs. Madden always wanted one. I could tell, by the way she looked at me.

Once, when it was hot and sticky, and I was on my way home from the pond, she invited me in. She was outside clipping her rose bushes with her big gloves on.

"You look warm young man, how 'bout a nice cold drink?" We had lemonade and chocolate chip cookies on her screened porch. That was nice. We didn't have a screened porch at our house. Besides I also got to see the inside of her house.

I visited Mrs. Madden many times after that. It was a new experience. Oh, I don't mean that I was the only kid in the neighborhood who had a real, grown-up private friend. I mean I felt something "new" about myself when I was with her. I felt my own margins, my own space. It was different from my space at home, which could be invaded by anyone, anytime. This one felt, well, safer, like Mrs. Madden wouldn't come inside my space without first asking me.

We sat there, me on the squeaky glider, and she in the tubular steel rocker. We talked about her Japanese beetles (they couldn't get through the screen), and my Catholic cousin, who was a Jesuit. We also talked about the books we'd both read: *Black Beauty, Pinocchio, Strongheart,* and then there'd be pauses, silences, spaces in our togetherness that felt just fine, not awkward like the pauses in conversations with other people.

One day I noticed a small statue on their mantelpiece. It was Pinocchio. "I've read that book!" I exclaimed, and then, as if that entitled me, "May I hold him?" I asked. I devoured Pinocchio with my eyes, the red feather stuck in his yellow cap, his big nose and oversized feet. I explored him with my fingertips: his smile, his hands, shyly hidden behind his back. My cheek told me he was cold.

Each time, after I'd visited Mrs. Madden, and Pinocchio, she'd put him back on the mantelpiece. How I wished she'd give him to me to keep. What would a woman her age want with a kid's toy like that, anyhow?

Maybe . . . maybe I could ask !

I began practicing. First I practiced on Patsy. She was the Covilles' dog. She was part German Shepherd and part Great Dane. She was really mine. She only ate and slept over at their house. My dad didn't like dogs.

We had a Mulberry bush in our side yard. Its branches were like a theatre curtain, cascading to the ground. You could pull the thick branches aside and go in and out of the darkened theatre-in-the-round. Patsy sat inside with her back against the gnarled trunk. She stared at me expectantly as I spoke, "Mrs. Madden, why don't you let me have that statue? I mean to keep! I'd take very good care of him."

"You know, Mrs. Madden, if you gave Pinocchio to me, you wouldn't have so many things to dust!" Patsy always said, "Yes," and licked my face. I practiced on the trees around the pond, and on a chipmunk or two. Finally, one day, I did it! As soon as she opened the front door I blurted it out, "Mrs. Madden I would like to have Pinocchio to keep, would you give him to me?"

"I certainly will," she said. "I thought you'd never ask. You know, son, if you ask, you sometimes get a 'yes'; but if you don't ask, you always get a 'no.'"

I clutched Pinocchio inside my T-shirt so he'd be safe until we got home. I kept saying to myself, "If you don't ask you always get a 'no'; but if you do ask, you sometimes get a 'yes'!" I did this so I wouldn't stumble; I was running so fast.

With Mrs. Madden, I had something special. No, I was something special. I had the best of both worlds; privacy when I wanted it, and togetherness when we both wanted that. She was neither too warm, too giving, nor too close, so that I felt suffocated. Nor was she too cold, too distant, or too preoccupied, so that I felt abandoned. She was J-U-S-T R-I-G-H-T.

We moved away when I was 13, and I never saw Mrs. Madden again. Sad. She doesn't know how very much she meant to me. She doesn't even know what else she gave me to keep for life, besides the little statue of Pinocchio. (And you know, I've often wondered whether or not she bought Pinocchio for me in the first place. I could swear it wasn't on her mantelpiece the first time I visited her. Seems to me Pinocchio showed up shortly after we'd talked about some of the books we'd both read when we were little.)

Guess I'll never know.

Perhaps there are other "Mrs. Maddens" among us. Maybe there are some of you who are completely unaware of how very much you have meant to someone whose life was once touched by yours.

Or, maybe, Mrs. Madden is like God!

Maybe you are like that, too … to someone.

Final Incarnation

ue called to ask me to help locate her son and tell him that her dad, his grandfather, had died. She wanted him to come to the funeral. Sue hadn't heard from him in months.

Wasn't hard to do. He was well known in the drug community in Washington. One in the morning. Near Half and "O" Streets SE. In the basement of an abandoned warehouse. It's called a "shooting gallery," because that's where folks gather to share needles and "shoot-up" heroin, PCP and cocaine.

Now, some parts of Washington are no place to be in broad daylight, much less after midnight. So I parked my car directly under a halogen street lamp. You learn to do this if you want your tape deck still in the dashboard when you return. I then walked several blocks to my destination.

It was very dark inside, and took a while for my eyes to adjust. The air was foul. Shadowy figures moved slowly about. Groans of pain and groans of pleasure mingled in the air. I asked one man if he knew where a twenty-year-old named "Bobby" was.

"Yes," he said, "over there."

I found him in a mild stupor, sitting up against one of the steel I-beams that held up the building. I tried to talk with him, but wasn't sure he understood me. I had typed him a note, which I stuffed into his jacket pocket.

After spending a little time with the dozen or so people in various stages of stupefication, I left.

As I was walking away from the building, I heard footsteps behind me. It was too dark to see who it was. I sped up. So did the other person. I was getting nervous, and then a voice called out, "Hi, Father, what are you doing here this time of night?" It was a policeman!

"Jesus and me got business in there," I said, as he fell in step with me.

"I'll walk you to your car," he offered.

"But you don't need to do that," I protested. "The Lord's never let me get mugged yet."

"Well," he said, "I hear he's kinda busy in Africa right now, so I'll just stick with you 'til you're on your way."

I thought that was a very gracious way for him to speak the truth about the precariousness of my situation.

As I pulled away from the glow of the street lamp and waved to him, I realized that once again, the Word of God's love had become flesh and dwelt among us, this time in the person of a D.C. cop who was also full of grace and truth.

Healing Service

I was conducting a healing service at St. George's for people with AIDS and their loved ones. After Communion, those who wished to could come up to the altar rail and whisper their concerns to the minister, and receive anointing and the laying-on of hands.

I noticed one young man when he first came in the door, wobbling, even with his cane. Almost six feet, and about 110 pounds. His face was covered with Kaposi's sarcoma lesions. He looked like he had chickenpox. When he came to the altar rail, he said, "I didn't come here to be cured of AIDS, I came here to be healed of self-pity."

I lost it at that point, but this was a safe place for that.

Christmas '92

ometimes, in the midst of all the excitement of the Christmas season, we forget what we're so happy about. We forget the "reason for the season," as the saying goes.

Some years ago, I was sitting in my counseling office in-between clients. The phone rang. It was Scott. I'd been visiting him for several weeks in the hospital.

"Jim," he said, "please come see me."

"Okay Scott, it's one o'clock. I've got two more clients today, but I'll be there by 4:30."

He paused, then said, "Come as soon as you can."

I walked into his room at 4:25. I spoke to him. He didn't answer. He'd apparently died in the past few minutes. I administered last rites, but I felt awful. He was certainly more important to me than those two client hours. I simply did not pay attention to his "pause." I didn't "hear" him when he asked me to come "as soon as you can."

How do I live with that negligence? That insensitivity? It was too late to correct it. I could barely drive home. I barely made it through the memorial service; looking at his file folder in the office; meeting members of his family; seeing the obituary in the paper; his photo. How do I live with this one? I don't. Nobody does. Some things we have to turn over to God, because we simply cannot deal with them.

And then somehow we are empowered to transform tragedy into blessing.

Now, whenever I get a call from a seriously ill person, I drop what I'm doing and go. Even if I just get an intuition about one of my clients or parishioners, I stop what I'm doing and go!

Maybe that was Scott's gift to me. So I might not have to go through anything like that again. Or, maybe it was his gift to others whom I might serve, after him.

We give thanks for you, Scott.

Sermon

"**H**eavenly Father, where we are wrong, make us willing to change. And where we are right, make us easier to live with!" Amen.

The purpose of having made a mistake is celebration! To celebrate our new learning for future reference. So we don't do the same dumb things over and over again. I was certainly not the best father in the world to our two sons. If I had it to do all over again, I wouldn't make the same mistakes twice. I'd make a whole brand new set of mistakes!

Mistakes are not for feeling shame or guilt. That's a waste of time. We were *built* to make mistakes. It's in our DNA. We were programmed by God to make mistakes. In our Baptism covenant, the Prayer Book doesn't say *if* we fall into sin but *whenever we fall into sin.* No 'ifs' about it. God knows that we will screw up, over and over again.

When Johannes Brahms finished one of his great symphonies, it was first performed in the Vienna Opera House. A young guest conductor was selected for the privilege of being the first to conduct Brahms' magnificent new work. Brahms himself was in the audience. When it was over, it was as if the applause would never end. At the reception afterward, the young conductor came up to Brahms and said, "I made a few changes in your composition Maestro, and wondered what you thought of them."

"Brilliant!" Brahms exclaimed, "but don't do it again!" He didn't jump on the young conductor's case and berate him for the arrogant impudence of presuming to improve on the master's work. He didn't put the young man's musical career in the trash can in Vienna (which he could have done in a heartbeat). He just said, "Don't do it again." That's what Jesus said, remember, to the woman taken in adultery? (Men, of course, couldn't commit adultery according to Jewish Law.* Just women! I wonder who the men were doing it with, if not with women?)

---

*My lawyer friend says that I'm "technically" wrong here. ...Yet, when was Jesus always "technically" right when he was making an important point?"

Anyhow, in John 8: 3ff, the Pharisees, an all-men's group, brought a woman to Jesus and said to him, "Master, this woman was taken in adultery, caught in the very act." (You didn't know they had peeping-tom's in the New Testament did you?)

"Caught in the very act" means somebody must have been peeking doesn't it? People don't usually commit adultery on the street corner! The group continued, "Moses in the law said that she should be stoned to death. What do you say?" Jesus didn't respond. He simply squatted down on the ground at the woman's feet, and doodled in the sand with his finger, as if he hadn't even heard the question. Jesus was so embarrassed for her that he knelt down and busied himself, so as not to further humiliate her.

The Pharisees bugged Jesus to answer them until he finally stood up and said that now-famous sound-byte, "He that is without sin among you, let him cast the first stone."

And he stooped down again and doodled in the sand. The crowd dispersed as it is written, "One by one, from the eldest to the youngest."

Now, why do you suppose the older people headed out first? That's because we older folk have had more chances to do dumb things than our younger counterparts. Jesus was now alone with the woman. Everyone else had sneaked off. He stood up again and, looking around and seeing no one, said to her, "Woman, where are your accusers?"

She said, "No man accuses me now lord."

And Jesus said to her, "Neither do I condemn you. Go, and sin no more." No recriminations about what she had done. No guilt tripping. "That was then," Jesus implied, "this is now." Just, "go and don't do it again." No making up for past mistakes. No confession. No penance. No shaming for her old behaviors. Just go. And don't do it anymore.

St. Paul knew what to do with his bad behaviors (including being a serial killer himself). He said, "This one thing I do, *forgetting those things which are behind,* and reaching forth unto those things which are ahead, I press on to the prize of the high calling of God in Jesus Christ." (Phil 3:13)

As you may know, much of my ministry the past 40 years has been devoted to pastoral counseling. Now, what is the one thing that keeps therapists in business? Guilt! People's shame for past mistakes. Remorse and humiliation for secret sins. Regret and fear of discovery and disgrace. Things Jesus never focused on. He focused on healing and new life, in spite of past mistakes. That's the good news.

If we could eradicate guilt from American culture, as a counselor I'd have been out of a job. The only thing guilt is good for is the mental health industry!

So, we can get on with it and go, "take on the day." That's the modern vernacular for, "Let the dead (past) bury itself."

For, "Lo, I am with you always," Jesus promised us. ... No matter what we've done. However, you and I know that the reality is that we will go and "do it again," and again, and again. So, how many times can we get away with this? Sin and be forgiven? At least 490 times according to Matthew 18:22, for starters. And, at four hundred, ninety-one, then what? God is still forgiving. You see, when God forgives, God forgets. When you and I forgive, we remember, and keep on reminding other people of their past errors, for the rest of their lives: "Now Johnny, remember what happened last time!"

We never let them forget.

Aren't you glad salvation is not dependent on one of us? But on a power much higher than ours, that supports us in getting through this world . . . one day at a time ... one sin at a time.

You don't have to be stuck in some dark past moment in your own little private autobiography. God don't make no mistakes.

Not even you! ... Not even me!

"You screwed up, but I love you anyhow." Amen.

Commander Wright

When I was a kid, everybody in our neighborhood knew Commander Wright. In those days, a commander was a big deal. There weren't many around. Especially any who'd been to the South Pacific on his very own battleship!

He was an imposing man; well over six feet, with a shock of white hair. He was also quiet, and very economical with words. He didn't speak unless he had something significant to say. Consequently, whenever he looked like he was about to open his mouth, everybody stopped chattering and paid attention to him. You had to. He never repeated himself. His quietness left a lot to the imagination. Some people thought he was grumpy. That's because he wouldn't talk nonsense with them.

He lived with his wife at the corner of Glebe Road and Twenty-fifth Street, in what must have been one of the original Aladdin pre-cut homes. It was very well built. And his yard was always trimmed, as if readied for inspection. He had a workshop in his garage. You could tell by the noises you heard in there as you passed by. I passed by a lot. I lived two houses away. Our house was a Sears Catalog bungalow, stucco.

One day the overhead door was up, and I could see in. I wanted to go look, but what if he chased me away? I crept along the privet hedge by the driveway. His back was to me. He was ripping a two-by-six in half and making too much of his own noise to hear me. I ventured closer, reminding myself that surely a United States Navy Commander wouldn't kill a twelve-year-old, fellow American citizen for trespassing. He cut the table-saw off and, without turning his head, addressed himself to the piece of wood he'd just cut and said, "Hi Jim, c'mon in."

I followed him around the shop and watched everything he did. I had a thousand questions that I dared not disturb him with. I thought I smelled coconut oil. Coconut shells! Hundreds of them, hanging from the garage rafters. I wondered how he brought back all those coconut shells in his ship. "Anything you want to ask I'll try to answer," he said.

How'd he know what I was wondering about? That was another question I didn't dare ask him. That was when I decided he was a mind reader and, besides, he had magical powers.

That summer he taught me how to build birdhouses out of coconut shells. I broke the first shell I tried to work with. It bounced on the concrete floor and shattered. I knew he couldn't go back to Hawaii to get more, being retired and all. I didn't even know where Hawaii was except he once said, "That way!" and pointed in the direction of Cohen's Grocery Store.

I stood there and waited to be yelled at, or hit, and hear, "You stupid kid, what'd you do that for? Can't you ever do anything right? After all I've taught you, and you pull a dumb trick like this? Why don't you just run along home until you grow up?" He must have heard it fall and crack open. All he did was reach for a new shell, mumbling, "They break easily, Jim, until you get the knack of it." (Now that's a new way to talk to kids, I thought to myself.)

Up until now, he'd been doing all the big cuts with the electric band saw for me. Today, he studied me carefully, from my Buster Brown shoes to my Vitalis-slicked hair and said, "I think you're big enough to learn how to use this machine yourself." I felt like I was a hundred-feet tall. He started by taking the machine apart, showing me how it was made, and then putting all the pieces back together again in sequence. He also told me how easy it was to cut off your own thumbs and fingers if you weren't careful.

I practiced on small pieces of white pine until I could zip off curves and angles like a pro. Then I attempted to cut my first coconut shell. I guess my excitement overcame my recently-informed good sense. I pushed the curved brittle shell into the blade too fast. There was a loud "snap" and the shell bounced off the far wall. The motor raced and something made an awful whine. Commander Wright moved like lightening to switch it off. "Are you hurt?" he asked.

"No sir."

"Good, your body is more valuable than all the machines in this shop." I began to tote that up to get an indication of my net worth!

Now, he'd already told me once not to put curved pieces to a band saw unless they'd been stabilized. But all he said was, "I guess it's time to show you how to fix a broken blade." He got out the welding equipment. Together we brazed it, cooled it, filed it smooth, and soon we were in business again.

I remember the first Wren house I successfully completed, all varnished, with a wire loop on top to hang it in our sour-cherry tree. My mother "oohed and aahed" over it but nobody, nobody knew what went into the making of that little birdhouse. Nobody except Commander Wright and me.

That summer we built several birdhouses. To an outsider, it probably looked like we were just building birdhouses. But we were also building something so much more valuable.

He taught me what it means to be "special" to someone, to make mistakes together in the process of getting better. He built into me some new convictions which have stayed with me and blessed my life and work ever since.

The first is that mistakes are for learning, and for celebration of that new learning. Mistakes are not to feel bad about, to feel guilty over. And the second is that people are more valuable than anything else.

As Reuel Howe, my professor at Virginia Seminary, once said, "We were intended by God to love people and to use things; but we end up using people to get the things we really love."

Alan

eing 14 and Gay in North Carolina was a bad combination for anybody. Alan's dad was a truck driver, so he was away from home a lot. Even when he was home he wasn't 'there,' at least not for the kids. They went to the Wesleyan Church on Sundays. Alan remembers Sunday mornings sitting in the pew listening to that little old man up there and thinking, "It sounded like I was in trouble." The sermons often reminded the congregation that homosexuals were the "scum of the earth, and a stench in the nostrils of God."

"The pastor was actually the head of our household, too. In that denomination, we couldn't dance, sing in the glee club, salute the flag in class, and no birthday parties."

One Sunday afternoon, he "confessed" to his parents that he thought he might be a homosexual. He said that he was more attracted to his male friends than the girls in school. They immediately drove him to their pastor's home. The pastor interrogated Alan, demanding all the embarrassing details. The reverend told his father to "take this boy home and beat the sissy out of him." Dad followed the pastor's instructions. The next day at breakfast, they demanded to know if he'd repented. Alan burst into tears and said, "I cain't he'p it mom, I just cain't he'p it."

His mother left the room and returned with a piece of paper in her hands. She held it over the huge glass ashtray on the coffee table and lit it with her husband's cigarette-lighter. It was Alan's birth certificate.

Finally, at 16, Alan felt that he had nothing else to lose. He took the Trailways bus to D.C. He'd saved enough money from doing yard work for the ticket and sandwiches. In the D.C. bus station, he found the *Washington Blade,* a free gay newspaper. He was amazed that there were others like him in the world.

It was Saturday night. He visited his first gay bar, one of nine in the city! It was dark, and noisy, and filled with smoke. He had no idea how to proceed.

He saw some men in leather jackets at the pool table. He got a soda and inched toward them. He watched them play for awhile. One of the men winked at him, and offered to teach him how to play. Later, he asked Alan to come to his place for another drink. Alan's new friend offered to teach him the "ropes"—literally! While Alan was nude, and tied down on the bed, his "teacher" raped him. Alan's cries were to no avail. A couple of hours later, he did it again. Then he untied Alan and pushed him out the front door with, "You'll get used to it kid."

Alan took the first local bus he found. It was marked "Springfield." He was bleeding from the assault and frightened, numb with disbelief. He saw a lighted sign in front of a Methodist Church. It gave the name and phone number of the pastor. Even though it was 3 A.M., he was desperate so he called. He woke the minister and, in-between sobs, told him what had happened.

It freaked out the clergyman, who said, "I don't believe I can help you, but there's a pastoral counselor in Fairfax who volunteers at the Whitman-Walker Clinic." He gave Alan my number and said, "Why don't you call him?"

I drove to meet him in front of the Mayflower Motel. Alan would not see a doctor. He was too embarrassed, so I took him to the home of a gay RN who worked at the clinic, and he took care of the damage. He also gave him the names of some friendlier contacts in the city.

Twenty now, Alan was sick. And scared. In desperation, he phoned his home. "Mom I'm sick. I have AIDS and the doctor says I might not live another year. If ever I needed you, it's now."

She hung up on him.

The gay men's clinic had a "Buddy System" made up of straight and gay men who took over his care as his condition worsened. He died five months later of pneumocystis carinii pneumonia. He strangled to death on his own spit. That's what PCP means.

On our last visit, Alan asked me to pray with him. He asked for a prayer of thanksgiving. "Thanksgiving?" I wondered, "for what?"

Souvenirs

"You're sick as a dog and you're grateful?"

He said that he was thankful for finally finding people who loved him; that he was loved, lovable, and that he was worth knowing. He didn't get this from his old church. He'd received it from a few men who, long ago, had had contact with Christ's One, Holy, Catholic and Apostolic Church.

The words were fuzzy: "For minds to think, and hearts to love, and hands to serve.

We thank you, Lord Jesus." (BCP p. 837)

Mae

I remember one rainy afternoon in 1975. I was going through some old family papers and came across a packet of report cards. They were from Bill's high school days. Bill lived with Nancylee and me as his legal guardians until he graduated from high school, and the insulting dependency of adolescence. He went on to graduate from Colorado University.

As I shuffled through the cards, I found a "C-" for one course with a note from his high school teacher: *Dear Mr. Petty: Bill is capable of much better work than he is doing.*

I wrote back: *Dear Madam: I am relieved to hear that Bill does have the capacity for doing better. I was beginning to think there was something wrong with him. Cordially, Jim Petty.*

Next semester it was a 'B+' with a note: *Dear Mr. Petty: this 'B+' could have been an 'A.' Bill is not working up to his full potential.*

Dear madam: I spend most of my time at the counseling center, trying to get people to slow down so they don't die prematurely of high blood pressure and heart attacks. I'm delighted to hear that Bill is learning about this so young. Cordially, Jim Petty.

Next time she wrote to me (there was no "Dear" on this one): *Mr. Petty! Bill does not always follow instructions, nor does he always do what he is told to do.*

I responded: *Dear Madam: Your notes are always so encouraging. We have been deeply concerned that we do not spawn robots instead of children. We have worked hard to encourage independent thinking and action in our children and are delighted to hear that you have noticed the results of our efforts. Keep up the good work! Most cordially, Jim Petty.* Bill must have done better the rest of his high school career because his teacher didn't write me any more notes.

As I sat on the floor staring nostalgically at those report cards, my mind wandered back to my own school days.

I was raised in Arlington, Virginia. I hated school from the first day of the first grade to the last day of the twelfth. In my case, the thirteenth. I was in summer school for twelve consecutive summers. It wasn't until the fourth grade that I found out it wasn't supposed to be that way. I was in a "year round" school program 30 years before it was conceived! I had a specially focused antipathy for mathematics, so I memorized my multiplication tables backwards . . . in reverse. My teacher never figured it out. In those days they were not allowed to hit us. But that did not deter the principal of John Adams grade school, Miss Mary Barber, from dragging me out of the classroom into the hallway several times a week and shaking me by the shoulders 'till I thought my head would snap off and roll down the corridor for her. I don't know why she bothered to take me out into the hall to do it. She yelled loud enough for all the world to hear, "Jim Petty, if you don't learn your tables, you'll never amount to anything!"

So, I spent the rest of my school career proving she was right!

Finally, they threw me out of the Arlington county public school system altogether. My parents had spent enough on private tutors to build a swimming pool, and now they had to pay to send me to Western High School in Washington, the only place left that would take me.

The bus let us off (I wasn't alone) every morning on the other side of Key Bridge. Now, you know what's on the other side of Key Bridge? The C&O canal. And that's where I spent most of my high-school career. On it, in winter ice skating; in summer, floating; or by it, fishing, in-between seasons.

I remember the day Franklin Delano Roosevelt died. It was April 12, 1945. I was sixteen, and sitting in class. Geometry I think, because the teacher was drawing dirty pictures on the board, "Elliptoids" or something. Suddenly, the intercom speaker hummed on and Principal Pawlowski's voice droned into the room, solemnly announcing the death of the president, and the closing of school for several days, "Beginning now!"

I gave a whoop of delight and tore out of the room.

The following Monday, I was summoned to the vice principal's office (he's the one in charge of "vice"). "March yourself right down to the guidance counselor's office, young man," he commanded. I figured I was in for some more "guidance," like I just got two weeks before. That was when he announced to me that I was not "college material" and that I should drop out of the academic program and get into the apprentice/trade training program, which included a part-time job. A very helpful man, he'd even picked one out for me and had arranged for an interview. It was with a septic tank cleaning company in Fairfax. They go around with a big truck and hose, and suck things out of people's septic tanks every couple of years. That seemed to me a distinct improvement over the classroom, so I'd told him I'd think about it. But that wasn't what he wanted this day.

When I walked in, he looked at me over his half-moon reading glasses, with real hate flashing in his eyes. I always had him figured for a hit-man for the Mafia after he retired anyhow. He jumped up, ground his fists into his littered desk top, and screamed at me through clenched teeth, "James Petty, you have no respect for the dead!"

"I do too!" I blurted back. "The very afternoon he died, I caught three catfish and I named the biggest one 'Franklin,' in his honor."

Well . . . somehow, I continued in the academic program, wintering in steam-heated D.C. classrooms; and summering in Virginia's sweltering ones.

Finally, graduation day came. They gave me a robe and a black hat with a tassel on it, and a rolled-up piece of paper tied with a red ribbon. All the other seniors had diplomas. Mine was a blank sheet of white paper. That was so I wouldn't feel "different" when I walked across the stage while everybody clapped. I don't think I was embarrassed; I had already broken some sort of record. I had the lowest grade-point average of the whole school. I'd flunked Algebra three times, and English twice, but they wouldn't give up. I'd have to go to Washington-and-Lee High School one more summer and at least pass senior English with a "D-" to get a diploma.

Back in Arlington again, just where I started out.

A couple of weeks after the graduation exercises, I showed up for summer school English class. I was late (as usual), had "forgotten" my notebook (as usual); I sauntered in with my defiant you-can-make-me-go-to-school, but-you-can't-make-me-learn-nothin' attitude; and, with as much noise as possible, made my way to an empty seat in front. I dropped into my chair and began my vigil, clock-watching. You may be too young to remember, but in those days the big hand would suddenly spasm forward to the next one-minute mark with a loud "click," and when it had done it fifty times, you knew the class was over.

This teacher was young, in her early 30s, and very pretty. She was about 5' 8", with black hair, and long, curved fingernails painted dark red. That was the rage in the 1940s. "Must be a new teacher," I thought to myself. "All she did was smile when I came in late. She didn't even chew me out in front of the class. Man, she's gonna be a pushover."

Her name was Mae Van Meter. After a couple of futile attempts to get me to "contribute" to the class, she volunteered to help me after school. I stage-whispered to the guy across the aisle, "That's all they teach 'em at Wilson's Teacher's College: 'Stay after class, Jimmie, stay after class.'" When they learn to say it right, they get a teaching certificate."

When the room emptied, I strolled up and sighed myself into the slat-backed oak chair beside her desk.

And then, "it" happened!

I met my match.

She picked up a file folder with my name on it, saying, "These are your school records Jim, from D.C. and Virginia." It was very thick. And then as if it were last week's newspaper, she threw it in her brief case, looked me straight in the eye, and said, "I don't need all that stuff . I just want to get to know the real Jim so we can work together this summer."

To this day, I don't know how she did it. Before I realized what I was doing, I heard myself telling her about my interest in music, how I could play the piano; and do carpentry, making sawhorses and doghouses; and growing things in the backyard. It felt weird telling a school teacher all these personal things. I think it was her eyes, limpid pools of bottomless blackness. They seemed to look right inside of me, and they seemed to see something in there that they liked. God knows what! She helped me get ready to do a grammar exercise on the board for the next class. Every day she stayed with me for an hour after school. One afternoon, I noticed her husband waiting for her in their car in the parking lot. I talked to him once. He didn't seem to mind her staying after for me. He just read the paper until she came out.

By the end of the summer, I had earned an "A-" and boy did I e-a-r-n it! That woman never gave anybody anything they hadn't worked for. When my dad saw my report card he literally had to sit down. There'd never been an "A" next to my name on anything before. My mother cried. And then she did what she always did when she didn't know what else to do, she baked a chocolate cake. For my teacher.

My life changed radically after that. Here was a person who was not a neighbor or friend who would not let what was bad about me totally wipe out what was good about me. Mae saw me the way God saw me.

That September, something arrived in the mail addressed to me. It was rolled up in a plain brown wrapper with no return address on it—like the old sepia naturist magazines used to come so your parents didn't know what you were getting.

It was my high school diploma. It was the first thing I'd earned in my life. Or maybe it was the first time in my life I thought anything was worth earning.

A few years ago, I ran into my old grade school principal, Miss Mary Barber. Remember her? The one with the "shakes"? It was in a restaurant in Alexandria. I'd just dropped in for lunch. I was wearing my clerical collar, having just come from making a hospital call. She was sitting alone at a table. I went over and said, "Hi."

She looked up at me, and in shocked disbelief exclaimed, "Why James Petty, what are you doing dressed up like that?"—as if I were going to a masquerade ball or something. I told her I was an Episcopal priest, had made honors in two universities, held three degrees, and was in charge of a rather prestigious congregation in one of the wealthiest counties in the state of Virginia. At that point, her elbow bumped her cup of tea off the table and onto the floor.

As I bent down to pick it up for her, she said, "Weren't you lucky, Jimmie, to get such a good job?"

I stood up, smiled and said, "No ma'am, they're lucky to have me." And I walked away. I walked away from a lot of things in that moment.

I often think of Mae Van Meter, with love. I will never forget her. She gave me the gift of a new sense of direction in life. One that multiplies and shares itself over and over again, like all of God's gifts seem to do.

And I will never forget the day I brought that report card home. I've never seen such excitement around the house. You'd have thought it was Christmas, or something.

And, maybe it was. It kind of felt like a new birth for me.

How else does the love of God get through to people, except in the person of someone who dares to love another human being, the way God loves everybody.

Humor

"Grant O God, that we may always be right, for thou knowest we will never change our minds."

—Old Scottish prayer

Calling

ears ago, I found my first baby picture in our family scrapbook. Old Doctor Sylvester was holding me in his left arm while trying to wipe off his glasses with his green scrubs using his right hand.

"Why is he cleaning his glasses?" I asked mom.

"Because you baptized him on your way into this world! I guess you were meant to be a minister!"

Is that what it means to be "called, from my mother's womb?" (Isa. 49:1)

Blessed Virgin Mary

I met Claude, an Anglo-Catholic, in my dorm at Virginia Seminary. He was flamboyant, and very funny. I always liked him. His sense of humor made up for its deficit in the rest of the junior class. He had a lovely, etched glass statue of the Blessed Virgin, about two feet tall in his room. He kept her on a shelf just above the prayer desk in the corner. At her feet, a beautiful blue votive candle burned.

One night, Claude invited a couple of us to his room, along with Sally Lee, the seminary hostess. He locked the door, broke out four exquisite French crystal wine glasses, unscrewed Mary's head, and filled our glasses with gin … from her belly!

Bonnie and Sarah

*S*aturday. Nancylee's on duty at the hospital today. When she came in to kiss me goodbye early this morning, she whispered, "A baby Mockingbird's fallen out of the nest in the Maple tree. Maybe you can get it back before it gets hot today."

It was my chance to sleep late, but I tossed and turned, worrying about that baby bird. I'd heard that if human hands touch it, the mother bird would abandon the baby. So I rolled out of bed, found a pair of surgical latex gloves, and started looking in the bushes that separated our house from the house next door. Bonnie and Sarah had bought the house several years ago. Nice women. They both worked for the government. Quiet neighbors. Kinda homebodies.

I worked my way down the backyard to where the bushes stopped and the two backyards are open to each other. Bonnie and Sarah had a picnic table down there, and often had coffee there in the mornings. Suddenly, I realized they were there. Bonnie was sitting at the table, and Sarah was leaning over her, hugging and kissing her—on the lips—for a long time. Sarah caught me in her line of vision and gasped. Here I was, in my jockey underwear and surgical gloves, in the bushes at dawn. I tried to explain that I was looking for a baby bird that had fallen out of its nest. Both were standing by the fence now, staring at me. Somehow I didn't feel believed.

Finally Bonnie said, "Well Jim, we won't tell, if you won't."

"Deal!"

Awards Dinner

y pastoral counseling office was in the Colonial Heights Presbyterian Church, right next to the parish hall. You had to walk through the parish hall to get to my office.

The women of the church were having an awards dinner this particular evening, and the banquet tables were set up with flowers and candles.

Marie was my last client for the day. She had been abused as a child by her father and was just becoming aware of it. To help her uncover the repressed memories, I asked her to picture her father's face on the big red plastic pillow on the floor in front of her. She knelt there quietly for a moment, and then suddenly started hitting the pillow with all her might, screaming, "Keep your hands off me! Don't touch me! I hate you! Stop that—you animal!"

By the end of the session, she said that she felt better than she had in years. I closed my attaché case, opened my door, and together we entered the parish hall. Eighty-five women sat at the banquet tables in silence, staring at us. Glaring at me. We walked down the aisle between the tables and headed for the parking lot. It was like a silent Ash Wednesday procession.

Next morning, Ed Hughes, the pastor, called me on the phone.

Women

he year was 1974. It was a very hot July day in Philadelphia. I took a puddle-jumper from DC to the church in this "city of brotherly love."

That's where the "Philadelphia 11" women were to be ("irregularly") ordained priests in the Episcopal Church. Riots were anticipated. Fire hoses were laid out, and mounted policemen patrolled the streets near the church.

I knew I was not supposed to go there. Wondered if I could be deposed from the ministry by the bishop when I got home. No matter. Alison Cheek and I were pastoral counselors together in Washington and I loved her. I even brought along a small pack of Ex-Lax for her 'irregularity!'

The church was packed. The ordination service was moving and exciting. The usual spot in the service for 'objections' was filled with some emotionally charged conservative Episcopalians. This was the moment of truth. Were these bishops going to go through with it in spite of risks to their own ordination, or were they going to knuckle-under and stop the service? We all listened intently to the objections. And then the bishop thanked them for their comments and calmly announced, "The service will proceed!"

The Holy Communion celebrated the presence of Christ, and the freedom of a new day for this church, beginning with that service.

It always takes a courageous few to move an institution off its fears. Now the church was in a dilemma. There were 11 women walking around in clerical collars, "irregularly," but not illicitly, ordained. Soon the irregularity was replaced with acceptance.

I puddle-jumped back to Virginia in time to get to the clergy conference with Bishop Hall. Nervously, I looked for him when I joined the group, but he was nowhere to be seen. Someone came up behind me and, slipping his arms around my chest, lifted me off the floor, (he was a big man) put his chin in my neck and whispered, "Did you have a good time in Philadelphia?" I knew I was home free.

After a stellar career, Alison retired. I hope you're well and enjoying yourself, dear Alison.

The Psalms

t announcement time, I asked the congregation to read Psalm 155 this week in preparation for next Sunday's sermon on the subject of lying, or telling falsehoods, in American society.

The following Sunday, when I got in the pulpit, I asked for a show of hands, "How many of you read Psalm 155 to get ready for today's sermon?" About half the congregation's hands went up.

"So much for my sermon on lying," I said. "There *is* no 155th Psalm!"

Retirement

 on't think I'll retire. I think I'll probably drop over dead, half way through some poor soul's counseling session ... and just hope they weren't coming to see me for abandonment anxiety!

Trust

"I lay my hands upon you praying: Abba, Father, ease the tensions of your body and set your mind at rest, that you may put your trust in one who is trustworthy. And I annoint and do sign and fix you with the sign of the cross, in sure and certain hope of the resurrection of the body, and the life everlasting. Amen"

Bonnell

I was drafted during the Korean War in 1951. The next year, on Thanksgiving Day, I was on duty at Camp Leonard Wood, outside Fort Monmouth, New Jersey. The post was deserted. Even though I was only a private, I guess I was "necessary personnel." I didn't mind. Army life was one of the best things that ever happened to me. That day though, I was bored, so I wandered into the post chapel. It was littered with service leaflets, but otherwise empty. So I just sat quietly in one of the pews. Suddenly, I was not alone. Nobody else was there. But I was not alone. It was a very powerful experience for me.

In the following weeks, I knew I needed a place, a church, in which to house this experience, but which one? I approached Chaplain Paul Klett, 1st lieutenant, Missouri Synod Lutheran, and took his "Doctrine of the Church" course. Next, I found Fr. Patrick Ryan and took the Baltimore Catechism class with him. Then Capt. Jack Baker, the Baptist chaplain. I had problems with all three. I had to agree with doctrines that didn't make sense to me at all, and yet, to doubt was sinful. I had to conform and be good ... and I knew I wasn't *that* good!

I began listening to *The National Radio Pulpit* on Sunday afternoons in the deserted barracks. Each Sunday, there was a different guest preacher: Norman Vincent Peale, Billy Graham, John Southerland ("Sib") Bonnell, Ralph W. Sockman, and others.

I liked Dr. Bonnell best. He ran the Fifth Avenue Presbyterian Church in New York City. So I called him, and said, "Hi, this is Jim Petty, I'm a soldier at Fort Monmouth. I like the way you talk. Can I come see you?" He agreed to see me. I borrowed the chaplain's olive drab staff car, and had no trouble finding the church. It was huge! Dr. Bonnell's mahogany desk was at least 15 feet long! But he didn't sit behind it. He came around and sat in a big wing chair just like mine. Close to me, and listened intently to my story. Finally, I finished.

He pressed his fingertips together and stared at the ceiling for awhile and then said, "Well, I suggest you take a look at the Episcopal Church. My guess is that that one would suit you best."

"Why?" I asked.

"Well, you're very bright and you're very kind, and a little bit of a snob!" He replied.

As we shook hands he said, "Do me a favor? Don't mention this meeting to anyone around here."

"Why not?" I asked, "it's been wonderful!"

"Well," he said, "not long ago, another young man sat in the same chair and told me about his conversion to Christ, and that he was also troubled about where to house his experience. I recommended he consider the Baptist Church. He sort of 'felt' like a Baptist, the way you 'feel' like an Episcopalian. And I'm concerned that my Board of Session might wonder why I didn't refer you both to the Presbyterian Church.

"Okay." I said, "I understand. By the way, what was the name of the other young man?

"Oh, his name was Billy Graham."

Ordination Day

I had graduated from seminary, and been cleared for ordination by the Diocesan Committees. The date was set. I called the bishop at Richmond before I sent out invitations, just to make sure of his intentions.

"I haven't decided yet," he said.

"Well," I asked, "should I buy my collar and clerical vestments?"

"I don't know," he said.

"But it's getting late to send out the invitations," I protested.

"Use your own judgment," he replied.

It was to be in the seminary chapel, on Saturday, June 16th. I was in my dorm, putting on my clergy vestments for the service of ordination. The seminary chapel bell tolled. My family and friends were already seated. I gathered up my cassock and surplice and new Prayer Book, and headed for the chapel. Bishop Goodwin was just ahead on the lawn, so I caught up with him and asked, "Bishop, when will I know if you're going to ordain me or not?"

Keeping his eyes straight ahead on the chapel door, he said, "Son, if you feel my hands on your head, then you'll know if I'm ordaining you today."

I did.

Encounter

ran a men's encounter group on weekends at our cabin in the Blue Ridge Mountains. Not very many weekends, however, because Nancylee and I enjoyed it too much ourselves.

American men tend to think tough most of the time, as a defense against their inborn humanity. So, one Friday night, after the men had all settled around the living room, their backs against huge Buddha pillows, I instructed, "No words now. No talk allowed."

I gave each of them a small bowl of chocolate pudding, paper napkin, spoon, a glass of water, and a straw. Then, I said, "You are to take turns feeding each other in absolute silence. Not too fast, not too slowly. Offer water when wanted or needed. Wipe mouths and chins as necessary. The only communication permissible is a nod or pointed finger to signal your wishes. When you finish with your partner, switch places. Fresh supplies are on the kitchen shelf."

Feeding, and being fed by another human being; having your wishes noticed; being totally responsible for another person for awhile; and having to submit to someone else, even temporarily. Becoming "as a little child again" in the evening; being touched by a stranger; letting yourself be cared for. It is powerful, profound, tender and complete. ... It's all there.

Our therapy session that night was pretty intense. When they were finally cocooned in their sleeping bags, scattered all over the floor, lights were out and you couldn't see your hand in front of your nose, all we could hear was the owls outside, and each other's breathing inside. As I dozed off, I thought I heard someone quietly weeping.

I called this exercise the Feeding Miracle. I picked it up from a guy named Jesus ben Joseph.

Goats

My orthopedic surgeon suddenly—it seemed to me—disappeared.

A letter turning his practice over to others didn't say why. He and Maryanne were members of my church. Seems he had a dream; a childhood dream of having a farm and raising goats. He'd loved the goats on a neighbor's farm when he was a child. Maryanne wondered why he subscribed to farm animal magazines.

He left a full and lucrative practice. His dad was a pediatrician and expected his son to go into medicine, which he obediently did. Maryanne had always dreamed of marrying a doctor.

And she didn't object to the financial lifestyle. Their divorce was eased by his having already turned over more than his share of their assets to her. They had no children, neither particularly wanted to.

He cashed in his part, packed a few things, and headed West. He bought a small farm in Iowa and started raising goats. There was a market for children, and adults, who were physically intolerant of cow's milk. He started cross breeding his goats, searching for one with a small frame, and a large udder that would produce high-fat milk. His medical knowledge was a big help in his new profession. He was with his beloved goats, and taking care of the medical needs of many more people than he used to.

When he developed just the right breed, he began shipping them to India, Africa and third-world countries. These animals ate less feed, were smaller to ship, and produced lots of high-quality milk.

He was, at last, a satisfied man who had followed his heart and trusted, even though it led him toward an uncertain future.

Kirk

When he showed up in my office this week, Kirk was very upset. He showed me the small, purplish lesion on his left arm and another on the sole of his right foot. The doctor told him he had maybe 14 months to live.

He talked about all the things he'd wanted to do and now never could. First on his list of dreams was to attend mass at St. Peter's Cathedral in Rome. He'd kept putting it off, but realized this was his last chance. Larry, his life partner, said, "Let's go! I can claim my six-month sabbatical at the university any time."

Kirk turned his car into Traveler's Checks and claimed his retirement assets.

They boarded the plane at Dulles. They began their tour of Italy, and loved it, but in a couple of months Kirk began getting sicker and sicker. They returned to the Vatican a few days before leaving for home.

Sunday afternoon, after Mass, Kirk sat in a wheelchair on the piazza, bundled up in a blanket even though it was summer. Larry went to get him a soda, but when he returned Kirk was gone. He died right where he most wanted to be.

Kirk lived more life in the past few months than most people do in a lifetime.

What a witness!

Maundy Thursday

*S*arah and Freddie had only been married for two years, and already she was sick of him. That's what brought them to my office. It wasn't that he'd been unfaithful, or wouldn't help with the dishes. He was just "there" all the time, and so goddamn "understanding" it made her sick. In all my born days, I've never met anyone as unexciting as Freddie. Sweet to a fault. Totally unspontaneous, he just stood around like a slightly nauseated puppy, waiting for Sarah to "do something." He never risked anything.

In short, he hadn't lived for 28 years. He'd lived one year, 28 times! Finally, in diagnostic frustration, I referred him to a clinical psychologist for a consultation. Fred was given a battery of tests. His profile on every one of them came back "normal." My consultant didn't have a clue about what to do with Freddie. Nor did I!

It was June. A thunderstorm arose. I half hoped the rain would discourage Freddie from coming. Yet in he walked, smiled gently at me, sat down and asked, "What you'd like to do this session?" He was a nice looking guy, bright, for a GS16, and most cooperative. I mustered a silent prayer, "God, help me with this one. Fred's not evil or bad or defective, just b-o-r-i-n-g." Then, I looked out the window onto Dolly Madison Boulevard. There were huge mud puddles all around the lawn. A construction crew was installing a new drainage ditch.

In a moment inspired by my own craziness, I spun around and ordered briskly, "Fred, take off your shoes and socks and roll your pants up to your knees, and come with me!" I modeled it for him. He looked at me as if I were the one who needed to be in a counselor's office, but, of course, he complied. He followed me barefoot out into yard, right into the center of a six-foot mud lake that was several inches deep. I began splashing my feet in the puddle and laughing, beckoning him to join me.

"My mother wouldn't let me do this, even with my rubber boots on," he said, as he gingerly stepped in.

I said, "C'mon Fred, it's fun." He did. Then I began singing, "Row, row, row your boat, gently down the stream, . . ." signaling him to join in.

Like a little boy, whispering because he was doing something naughty, he began quietly, "Merrily, merrily, merrily, merrily, life is but a dream," gradually increasing his volume under my imaginary conductor's baton. I laughed. He laughed (first time, ever). We both laughed, louder and louder like two rowdy kids. By now we were covered with mud. I grabbed his hands in mine and we danced around in a circle until the last "life is but a dream" came to a happy, wet end.

By now, we'd drawn a small crowd. The county road crew had migrated over toward us, like water buffalo chewing their cud and staring. "Guess we'd better get back to the office Fred," I said, as I put my arm around him and led the way to the church's garden hose. While we were washing the mud off each other's feet, I heard one of the laborers say to the others, "God! that was spooky."

Fred became much more interesting after that. In fact, this episode turned out to be only the beginning of many more of his forays into life, as if he were making up for what he didn't get to do when he was five. After he left that afternoon, I looked up the word "spooky."

It means "spiritual."

Family/
Community

"Lord, teach us to care and not to care."

—TS Eliot

Airlines

*R*ecently I saw, and greatly admired, a beautiful, multi-colored crocheted shawl in a boutique window. I thought Nancylee would like it for when we go to special places, like the Kennedy Center. But it was far too expensive.

"If I want that shawl bad enough, I can learn how to make one myself," I thought. So, I got the pattern instructions from the boutique lady, and a basic book on crochet. Wouldn't you know, it was French Filet—not the easiest stitch for a beginner. It took me a year to complete it. She loved it.

A few months later, we were on a plane to New Orleans for a pastoral counseling convention. I was practicing some crochet stitches to make cloths for car washing. A hefty, stubbled, red-haired man with a dead cigar butt hanging from his mouth passed up and down the aisle several times, sort of rotating himself around as he passed my seat. I'm sure it was so he could get a better look at me. Finally, he couldn't stand it any longer and blurted out, "What in the ha-il are you a' doin'?"

"It's called crochet," I informed him.

"Only sissies do that stuff. Why are you a' doin' it?" He asked.

"Well, I'm on weekend pass from Central State Mental Hospital," I said. "They put me in there because when I get upset I hurt people . . . real bad. The psychiatrist said that if I keep my hands occupied, it'll help me to control my violent urges."

For the rest of the flight, brother red-head didn't need to go to the bathroom anymore.

San Francisco

I'd never been to California. Couldn't imagine why anybody would risk earthquakes to go there. Maybe my clerical collar might somehow protect me from the tremors. I decided to go, not because my fear of earthquakes lessened, but because my wish to attend the first AIDS Conference at Grace Cathedral overrode everything else, temporarily. Enough, at least, for me to get on a plane with Nancylee.

We stayed over for a couple of days after the conference and did some sightseeing. We visited the Wharf, and its ethnic restaurants. Nancylee went to Ghiradelli's to buy some candy while I went to the restroom in the sub-basement of the skyscraper next door. I was standing at the urinal when I heard deep rumblings, and the building began to shake. In trance-like dread, I slowly, mutely, turned toward the nearest available human being. He was at the next urinal. I was going to ask if this were "It," if I was gonna die, down here in the bottom of this huge building, and Nancylee was going to die in the candy shop, separately. I opened my mouth, but nothing came out. I realized that I was urinating on his left pant leg. (You know how a sudden attack of fear can cause you to lose bladder control.)

Then the building trembled again. Well, *terror* shuts down the whole process completely! I remember moving as if sleepwalking, toward the door, opening it and slowly turning back to the man. I didn't know what to say. He was standing there, his gray pinstripe trousers turning charcoal from the knee down ... just standing there. I heard myself articulate a weak "thank you" to him. (What else do you say to someone you've just done that to?)

In a daze, I took the elevator up to ground level, amazed that it was still running! When I got to the door, I asked the guard, "What do we do now? The whole building shook a few minutes ago."

"Oh," he said, "that was BART, the Bay Area Rapid Transit going through the tunnel underneath the building."

I ran to look for Nancylee and found her sampling chocolates. Popping one in my mouth, she whispered, "Don't look now honey, but you've come unzipped."

She had no idea.

Grandma

randma was the only sane member of my family. One Sunday night, we were at her house for dinner. Her dog's name was "Fritzi." He was mostly a smooth-haired fox terrier, and "sumpin' else," as she said. I got to feed Fritzi his Red Heart canned dog food, which she kept in an icebox dish in the Frigidaire.

Mom and Aunt Rona and Aunt Lucy were there, too, carrying on in the living room while Grandma fixed baked meat loaf, mashed potatoes and gravy, and green beans for dinner. I helped her. Everybody remarked about the delicious meat loaf.

After dinner I helped Grandma clean up. She told me to feed Fritzi. When I opened the other ice box dish, the meat wasn't round, in the form of the can. It was flat and square. "Oops!" I said, and held it out for Grandma to see.

"Don't say anything," she responded, "they'll never know the difference. Just give Fritzi the ground hamburger."

Well, I never did tell up until now. They're all dead, including Fritzi, so it's okay to "tell."

The Reception

ancylee and I were at Grace Church, in Cincinnati, meeting with the altar guild lady to plan the reception for our wedding.

"Would you like pink champagne or white?" she asked.

"Neither," I said. "No alcoholic beverages."

"But it's not a *real* wedding without champagne!" she retorted.

"Then I guess our children will just have to be illegitimate, like Jesus was."

Gifts

One Saturday morning, Steve, our 11-year-old son, and I headed for our mountain cabin. Nancylee and his younger brother, Eric, would be up at dinnertime. Steve and I had just unpacked the car when we heard noises down at the foot of the hill ... like baseball bats smacking against the trees, and people yelling.

"Guess we'd better go investigate this," I said.

Steve countered, "Well, why don't you go, Dad, and I'll wait up here for you."

"But it's on our property, Son, we have a right to go check it out. Now come along." He followed, somewhat behind me.

As we got closer, we could see, through the trees, a bunch of teenagers, one beating a tree stump with a fallen branch, two others splashing bare-foot in the stream, and others running around yelling. They saw us first.

I yelled, "Hi!" They waved back. One girl asked if we lived in the "Chinese House" up there. (The cabin is up on posts.)

Turns out, this was the last day of school for the summer, and they were partying in the woods. The largest of the group was a young black man called "Junior." Nothing junior about him. He was six feet tall and about two hundred pounds. He chatted with us a bit, and then turned to Steve and said, "Hey, boy! You like to come wif' me? I'll show you sumpin' new." I watched Steve, hand-in-hand with Junior, disappear into the woods. I sat down on a fallen tree over the stream and listened to the kids talk about how it felt like being let out of jail for the summer. Nice bunch of young people.

Pretty soon here they came, Steve with a flowering plant in his right hand, and his left still in Junior's. Steve was grinning from ear to ear.

"What'cha got?" I inquired.

"A flower for Mom," he responded. We said our goodbyes, and as we trudged up the hill toward the cabin, Steve held firmly to his gift.

About half-way up, I suggested we rest for a moment and I said, "Steve, that's the way life is. Nine out of ten people mean you no harm. Only one out of ten is looking to harm you or take advantage of you in some way. Didn't you have a good time down there?"

"Yes."

"And you liked Junior, didn't you?" Steve nodded affirmatively.

"So," I went on, "you can't let fear of a few bad eggs keep you from enjoying the rest of the world."

Sermonette over, we made our way up to the cabin. Steve got a mason jar, filled it with water, placed the flower in it, and put it on the kitchen table. It had large, bright green leaves around a brown-and-green-striped "pitcher" blossom.

In a little while, Nancylee and Eric arrived and unpacked. Nan was just starting dinner when she asked me what was that peculiar smell in the house. I didn't know, but I heard someone making strange noises outside. When I poked my head out the door, Steve was almost doubled over, stifling laughter with his hand.

"Do you know what this stink is Steve?" I asked.

"Ha, ha, ha on you, it's a skunk cabbage!"

At least I don't have to worry about him not having a sense of humor.

Eric

We were at St. George's when Eric started first grade. I never wondered about the brakes on those yellow school busses until I saw the little feller trudge down the driveway toward one. He looked so small, and this step in his life felt sad . . . and happy, at the same time.

We were there waiting for him at three o'clock when he stepped down the big steps and the folding doors closed behind him. He slowly moved toward us, his head down, dragging his satchel in one hand and lunch box in the other. Not a happy camper this afternoon.

"How was school?" I yelled at him when he got within earshot.

"Awful!" he growled back.

Trying to be upbeat, as he got closer, I asked, "What did you learn in your first day of school?"

"I learned you can't call the teacher 'asshole,'" he said.

"Oh . . . that's a good thing to know."

Christmas

"Over the river and through the woods…"

I remember one Christmas Eve dinner when Nancylee's mom was visiting. Our eight-year-old son, Eric, adored mashed potatoes—even more than ice cream. Well, Grandma's fun, except the only time she listens is when she's not talking. And that's not too often!

First, Eric whispered in her ear, "Grandma please pass the potatoes." No luck. He raised the decibels. "Could I *please* have the mashed potatoes, Grandma?" To no avail. Finally, fairly yelling, "Would somebody please pass the fucking potatoes?" She heard that! Now she stopped talking, and passed him the potatoes with a critical glance at Nancylee and me, to which I responded, "Well, he did say 'please,' didn't he?"

Christmas '91

*T*he text is from the gospel according to St. John:

You shall know the truth, and the truth will make you free. (8:32)

One Thanksgiving, a young couple from up the street came to see me in the rectory at St. Andrew-In-The-Field. They had two small children and one shaggy dog, of mixed lineage. Every other year since her parents had retired to Florida, they piled the whole "family" into their VW Bug and drove to Pensacola, Florida, for Christmas. They really couldn't afford it, and the trip was agonizing, but they didn't want to disappoint the old folks who were living all by themselves. On alternate Christmases, the grandparents flew up and spent ten days in their tiny two-bedroom house, sleeping on the lumpy foldout bed in the living room.

The next summer, I attended a national Episcopal Church conference in Atlanta. At lunch, I overheard a rector from Pensacola talking about an older couple and their "problem." Several years back, it seems, they moved to Florida because he loved fishing and she loved boating. And, they had dreamed for years of attending the Christmas midnight mass at St. Peter's Basilica in Rome. But their obligation to their daughter, up in Maryland, came first; they didn't want to disappoint them. "They have a new baby you know," Grandma had explained.

During the break after the workshop, I sidled up to him and said, "I couldn't help overhearing your parishioner's Christmas pilgrimage problems. Tell me, what part of Florida do you hail from?"

"Pensacola," he said.

"And where does their daughter live?" I asked.

"Northern Maryland," he said.

"Hmm. ... Well," I said, "something tells me your parishioners will be in Rome this Christmas," and moved off before he could ask where I was from.

Unlike most other mental health professionals, pastoral counselors make house calls. So I made one.

That year, the young couple got a happy Christmas card from Rome. And I got a happy Christmas card from up the street. Truth does help.

Brotherly

*T*hen there was the Sunday afternoon we were all out foolin' around in Nancylee's new yellow Chrysler. As we passed the Baskin-Robbins 31 Flavors Ice Cream store, both boys yelled in unison, "I want ice cream!"

Nancylee pulled over, and I gave Eric the money for two cones. Steve called to him as he slammed the car door, "I want a chocolate cone, too!"

Pretty soon Eric appears. As he stepped off the curb he slipped, and one scoop fell out of its cone. Almost before it hit the hot asphalt, he moaned, "Aw Steve, I dropped your ice-cream cone!"

Samantha

*I*f any of us comes here to worship a God who sends people to eternal hellfire and damnation for overeating or having sex with the wrong person, listen up. Not that you can use the gospel as license to stuff your face with chocolate eclairs for breakfast, or be irresponsibly promiscuous and get away with it. But God doesn't have to punish you for these things. As it is written, "Verily, they have their own reward." I once went to my internist, who took one look at me and said, "Jim, you look like you're 'eight months gone!'"

So, if you want to keep on eating chocolate eclairs for breakfast, help yourself. God has bigger fish to fry. George Tittmann used to say, "God is not interested in your nasty little sins."

God is not some kind of cosmic voyeur sitting up there on the throne just waiting to catch us in some ... what shall we say ... "indiscretion." This kind of "God is gonna git'cha" school of theology doesn't help much when you already have enough guilt to last you the rest of your life, even if you never make another mistake.

Christianity sometimes gets reduced to such foolishness, and men are such fools to start with, that religion only compounds the problem. "Be nice, and say your prayers at bedtime; brush your teeth; stand up when they play the national anthem; wear your coat and tie to church; don't cheat on your taxes; and, when you die, you'll go to ... West Virginia!"

How far the church has strayed from the body of Christ sometimes taxes me beyond belief. Several years ago, a priest who had been in his parish for twenty-seven years was removed from that office, by his bishop, for allowing people to come to the Holy Eucharist in jeans and sweatshirts. "Oh this must have occurred in some place like Leningrad in the seventies, right?" How about Dayton, Ohio, in 1989! His bishop announced, "I only have pity for him, since he will have to face an angry Christ in judgment."

Do you really believe Jesus gives a diddily-squat what you're wearing this morning?

The problem is that we've confused American civil religion, and the punishment/reward behavior modification theory of modern psychology, with Christianity. And they are as different as chocolate eclairs and dill pickles.

Well ... let's talk about sin, since I seem to know so much about it.

I have a weakness—several actually—but a special weakness for auburn hair. I *love* the color of mahogany: to stare at it; run my fingers through it; and to "feel" the deep color with my fingertips. (That can get you in trouble at the mall!)

Nancylee and I were at the beach one summer, where I like to get up early, walk the shore, and watch the sun rise.

You know how you can sometimes sense when you're not alone? Well, I looked up and there she was: a vision of cinnamon-crowned beauty, sitting atop a sand dune. Her long, silky, auburn hair, flowing in the breeze, was silhouetted against the azure blue sky.

She had slender, graceful legs, glistening white teeth, and toes dug into the sand. I stood transfixed for a moment, and then moved toward that shimmering loveliness like a heat-sensing missile.

She was so regal sitting up there on the crest of the dune, a ten-foot rope around her neck, tied to a steel pipe hammered into the sand.

Her owner was sitting nearby eating a chocolate doughnut. I called ahead to her, "I just love Irish Setters!" which probably reassured her that I wasn't really staring at her doughnut. It did look good.

"Her name's Samantha," she called back to me. At the sound of my voice, the dog barked a friendly "hello" and, tail wagging, started running round and round, locked into a twenty-foot circle she'd made for herself. I sat and petted Samantha, and ran my fingers through her hair and hugged her. You could almost feel the color of auburn in her silky, satiny, soft fur coat. I watched the woman finish her doughnut. A chocolate one.

Then somebody down at the surf yelled, "Turn her loose so she can come to me!" It was the woman's man-friend, who was surf fishing. The woman unsnapped the rope from Samantha's collar and shouted, "Now you can call her!"

"Samantha, come here Samantha!" he called. The dog barked and started running excitedly around the twenty-foot circular rut she'd made in the sand. *She was free ... but she didn't know it.*

So she kept running around in circles, until finally the woman had to go over and take her by the collar and lead her down the sand dune towards her master. When the dog caught on that the rope no longer bound her, she raced straight to the fisherman.

We Christians have been so committed to an unforgiving, vengeful God, and to earning our own salvation, that God had to send Jesus to take us by the collar and lead us to the one who loves us more than anything else in this world. To the Father whose son still daily beckons, "Come unto me all ye who are sick and tired of being sick and tired, and I will refresh you." If necessary, I will come down to where you are and personally lead you to the Father.

Some of you may remember the 1960s (then) contemporary folk masses, rock operas, and modern "mystery plays." In the final act of one such play, a young man comes out, in pure white Eucharistic vestments and dirty tennis shoes, carrying a big book entitled *The Gospels*. He solemnly opens it, and reads in a loud voice, "You screwed up, but I love you anyhow."

He closes the book, chanting, "The gospel of the Lord." And in a way that condenses what all four books of the Gospels are trying to say in one sentence. "You screwed up, but I love you anyhow." Screwing-up we understand.

It's the "I love you anyhow" part of the good news that we self-sufficient westerners have trouble with. We don't want to be beholden to anybody.

But, as long as men prefer darkness to light (John 3:19), bondage is safer than freedom. So we have to tell the story over and over again until all of us recognize that we don't have to keep running around in circles of our own making; circles of crippling guilt for our nasty little sins. We have been freed from the law of sin and death, from bondage to our own guilt by the mighty act of God in Jesus Christ.

Stand fast therefore in the liberty wherewith Christ has made us free, and be not entangled again with the yoke of bondage. —From Paul's letter to the church in Galatia (5:1)

Amen.

Acknowledgements

Many folks have helped me in many ways:

Advised me to leave out the vignettes they liked least, and why.

Encouraged me to include the ones they liked.

There's no way I can name any without disappointing others. You know who you are and you know my appreciation. Someone once said something like, "It's amazing what can get accomplished in this world if we don't care who gets the credit."

About the Author

The Rev. Petty is an Episcopal priest. Prior to retirement in 1998, he was a parish clergyman; pastoral counselor in Northern Virginia and D.C.; a member and, later, chair of the Diocesan Commission on AIDS Ministry; founding board member of northern Virginia AIDS ministry; a member of the Rapid Response Team for the Diocesan clergy sexual misconduct task force; a volunteer therapist for the Whitman-Walker Clinic in D.C.; a Fellow in the American Association of Pastoral Counselors; and was on the staff of the Pastoral Counseling and Consultation Centers of Greater Washington.

Father Petty holds degrees from George Washington University and Virginia Theological Seminary (M.Div.). He completed his clinical pastoral residency at Bellevue Hospital in New York City. He is founding Vicar of St. Francis Church, Great Falls, Virginia.

Fr. Petty is living in retirement with his wife, Nancylee, in Black Mountain, North Carolina. They have two grown sons. Since moving to the mountains of Western North Carolina, they have attended Trinity Episcopal Church in downtown Asheville.

At my ordination on June 15, 1959, my rector, George Tittmann, said, "Today you are sent to comfort the afflicted, and afflict the comfortable."

Mission accomplished!